**Gowd Saraswat Brahmin's Cookbook by Annapoorna Nayak and Maya Shenoi**

# Limit of Liability and Disclaimer of Warranty

We have used our best efforts in preparing the Recipe Book, and the information is provided "as is." We make no representation or warranties on the accuracy or completeness of the contents of the cookbook and we specifically disclaim any implied warranties of merchantability or fitness for any particular purpose.

We are not responsible for the outcome of any recipe you try from this book. You may not achieve the results desired due to variations in ingredients, cooking temperatures, typos, errors, omissions, or individual cooking ability. You should always use your best judgment. You should always take care not to injure yourself or others on sharp knives or other cooking implements or to burn yourself or others while cooking.

You should examine the contents of ingredients before preparation and consumption of these recipes to be fully aware of and to accurately advise others of the presence of substances that might provoke an adverse reaction in some consumers, even if the recipe is marked as specific allergen free.

All material in the Recipe Book is provided for your information only and may not be construed as medical advice or instruction. No action or inaction should be taken based solely on the contents of this information; instead, readers should consult appropriate health professionals on any matter relating to their health and well being.

WE DO NOT CLAIM TO BE DOCTORS, NUTRITIONISTS OR DIETITIANS. THE INFORMATION IN THE RECIPE BOOK IS MERELY OUR OPINION AND DOES NOT REPLACE PROFESSIONAL MEDICAL OR NUTRITIONAL ADVICE.

In no event will we be liable for any loss or damage including without limitation, indirect or consequential loss or damage, or any loss or damage whatsoever arising from loss of health, fitness, data or profits arising out of, or in connection with, the use of this book.

# Social equality

We believe in social equality, where all people within a specific society or isolated group have the same status in some ways, often including civil rights, freedom of speech, property rights, and equal access to social goods and services.

This book is about the cuisine of a specific community called 'Gowd Saraswat Brahmin' (GSB). The mention of 'Brahmin' is not meant to bring attention to the caste system or glorify caste. GSB is more of a community rather than just a Brahmin caste. This community could hardly be a few hundred thousand in population. The point of this book is to document the culinary culture of this dwindling community. Such cookbooks not only help preserve our culinary history and food culture but they also help open up our unique way of life and share it with the world.

We do not intend to hurt the sentiments of any individual/group or organization, however we cannot be held responsible for the presence of any information that may upset or violate a particular custom or tradition, unknowingly.

# Dedication

This Book is primarily dedicated to my beloved Mother, from whom I learned the fun of cooking and also to the recipes that are all very traditionally Konkani.

Apart from my Mother, my gratitude and special thanks to my husband and children – Rajeev, Rahul and Shivika who helped to make this book a colorful one through their valuable inputs.

Special thanks also to the Co-author and my cousin - Maya Shenoi who gave all the encouragement and inspiration to be a part of this venture."

*- Annapoorna Nayak*

Dedicated to my parents and brother, for everything!

Special thanks to my cousins Anou Athri Vats, Ranjit Kamath and my sisters-in-law Sylvia Shenoi, Preeti Athri for their positive support and encouragement in order to make this book a reality!

*- Maya Shenoi*

# Notations

Vegetarian: All recipes mentioned here use only grains, pulses, nuts, seeds, vegetables and fruits, with the use of dairy products. This symbol will be marked on top of all vegetarian recipes.

Vegan: Some recipes mentioned here are vegan. They exclude anything of animal origin, including dairy products, honey, eggs and meat. This symbol will be marked on top of such recipes

Gluten Free: Most of the recipes mentioned here exclude gluten, a protein composite found in wheat, barley, and rye. This symbol will be marked on top of such recipes.

Nut Free: Most of the recipes mentioned here exclude nuts, which may have allergens that can be problematic to those allergic to nuts. This symbol will be marked on top of such recipes.

Low Fat: Quite a few of the recipes have extremely low fat and oil content. This symbol will be marked on top of such recipes

Quick: Quite a few of the recipes can be made in under 30 minutes if all ingredients are prepped and ready at the kitchen counter before preparation begins. This symbol will be marked on top of such recipes

# Measurement

| Measure | Equivalency |
|---|---|
| 1 teaspoon | 5 milliliters |
| 1 tablespoon | 3 teaspoons (15 milliliters) |
| 1/4 cup | 4 tablespoons (59 milliliters) |
| 1/2 cup | 8 tablespoons (118 milliliters) |
| 1 cup | 16 tablespoons (237 milliliters) |
| 1 bowl | 2 cups |

# Gowd Saraswat Brahmin's Cookbook

## Table of Contents

# History of Gowd Saraswat Brahmins

## Origins

According to one of the many theories about the origins of the Gowd Saraswat Brahmins (GSB); the 'Saraswat' term in GSB originates from 'Saraswati', the name of an extinct river mentioned in the Rig Veda and later Vedic and post-Vedic texts. This area was called the 'Saraswat Desh', and the Gowd Saraswat Brahmins claim their origin to the brahmins who lived here, on the banks of river Saraswati. They derived their name from either the river Saraswati or from their spiritual leader, the great sage Saraswat Muni, who lived on the banks of river Saraswati. The details mentioned hence-forth are collected from the noting in the internet. Some is mythology and some is historical and geographical documentations. As with any mythology, there is not much scientific evidence of this but we would like to believe that this could be the possibility of history of the Gowd Saraswat Brahmin community.

## Saraswati River

The Rigveda is an ancient Indian sacred collection of Vedic Sanskrit hymns. It is counted among the four canonical sacred texts of Hinduism known as the Vedas.

The Nadistuti Sukta "hymn of praise of rivers" is hymn 10.75 of the Rigveda. The hymn mentions river Saraswati to be between Yamuna in the east and the Sutlej in the west. Based on historical maps, archaeological sites, hydro-geological and drilling data, many scholars believe that major Indus Valley civilization sites lie along the river Saraswati. It is also believed that, on the banks of Saraswati River, the genesis of vedic sanskrit happened along with the writing of initial parts of Rigveda and several Upanishads, possibly in 2nd BC.

Many scholars have identified the Vedic Saraswati river with the Ghaggar-Hakra River, which flows in northwestern India.

## First migration~ 400-350 BC

The holy books of Hinduism like the Vedas, the Ramayana, the Mahabharata, the Bhagavata and the Bhavisyottara Purana have mentions of the Saraswat Brahmins in the story of great sage Saraswat muni, who was the son of sage Rishi Dadichi.

The lore goes to say that around 400-350 BC when the entire Saraswat Desh started becoming arid, the people had no means of growing their crops and had no choice but to migrate elsewhere. This period of history saw many civilizations abandoning their settlements. The migration happened over many centuries, the last of the exodus being around 350 BC due to a wide spread famine which lasted for 12 years. It is believed that the Saraswats mostly migrated to Sind, Kashmir and to Bihar around 400-350 BC. The place in Bihar where they migrated was Trihotrapura or modern Tirhut in upper Bihar or Gauda/Gowda desa, as it was called then. Some Vaishnava literature mentions Bengal as Gauda desha. It could have been the entire area in the Bihar and Bengal region.

In Bihar at that time, the Lichhavis were ruling, followed later by the Mauryas and then the Palas. After the Pala kings, around 1000 AD, with attacks from Mahmud Gazni, it is likely that the Saraswats moved to Goa. Since they migrated from the Gowda Desh, they were then named Gowda Saraswats, to distinguish them from other Saraswat groups of North. The migration from Bihar to Gomantak is recorded in the Sahyadri Khanda of Skanda Purana, an ancient Hindu text.

There is another interesting mythical folklore linked with the movement of Saraswats to Gomantak. In Tretayug, there was a Saraswat Brahmin named Rishi Jamdagni who was a great ascetic. He had a cow, known as a Kamdhenu because she was endowed with the power of fulfilling every wish. Once a king from Kshatriya (warrior) community, Sahastrarjun, had gone to the forest for hunting. There he found Jamadagni Rishi's ashram and went inside looking to rest. When he saw the cow, Kamdhenu, he expressed a desire to possess it but the Rishi declined to part with it. Then the arrogant king killed the rishi and took away the magical cow. The Rishi Jamdagni's son, Parshuram, was in the deep forest gathering wood for the yagnas, when came to know about the sad news. In his fury, he took a vow that he would annihilate all kshatriyas from this earth. He fought fierce battles to complete his vow and conquered their lands. He gifted the entire earth conquered by him to the brahmins. He went to the west of the Sahyadri mountain range, pushed the sea further west and created a new region, since it was not proper to live on the land gifted away by him. The land thus recovered, which stretches from Maharashtra to Kanyakumari, came to be known as Parashurama-kshetra. The recovered land is also known as Konkan or "corner of earth", ( Kona aka corner and kana aka piece).

Lore goes on that 96 families of Saraswat Brahmins, from Trihotrapura or modern Tirhut in upper Bihar & Bengal, which was known as Gowd Desh, were invited by Lord Parshuram to settle in the Gomantak region of the new region he had created; 66 (Sashast) in Salcette and the balance 30 (Tis) in Tiswadi. Thus they came to be known as Gowd Saraswat Brahmins. There is a view that these 96 settlements were referred as Sahanavis (Saha means six and Navi means ninety) and later as Shenvis. These settlers belonged to 10 Gotras - Bhardwaja, Koushika, Vatshya, Kaundinya, Kashyapa, Vasishtha, Jamdagni, Vishwamitra, Gautam and Atri.

In the course of time the families multiplied and with the passage of time they took to trade and commerce as permitted by the scriptures, besides officiating as priests. Depending upon their occupations this gave them various surnames as they have to-day like Kini - a treasurer handling money with the jingling sound, Mallya - a construction contractor who built mansions or mahals, Nayak-a leader in any army. In Goa they flourished and built hundreds of shrines and temples besides establishing Shri Kaivalya Math in the eighth century.

## The first exodus from Goa (14th - 15th century)

It is believed that around 13th century, the army of Tughlaqs of Delhi captured the Kadamba region, which included the Gomantak province. In the 15th century army of Bahamani sultan, a muslim ruler, attacked Goa. They destroyed many temples and the Hindus were forced to be converted to Islam. To avoid the religious persecution several Saraswat families moved south towards Kanara and a few went further down to Kochi in the Kerala Malabar Coast.

## The second exodus (16th century)

The migrations were happening in smaller numbers during the 13th, 14th and 15th centuries, but it became an exodus after the Portuguese came in the 16th century. In the early 16th century, the Portuguese general Alfonso Albuquerque captured Panaji and Portuguese rule was established. At first, the Portuguese did not interfere with the locals, although they banned the sati rite (burning of widows). They employed Hindus and engaged them in their armies, and they maintained good trade relations with the Hindu empire of Hampi. Around 1583, Christian missionary activities in Cuncolim led to conflicts. Around this time the Portuguese initiated the Goa Inquisition.

The Portuguese colonial administration enacted anti-Hindu laws to encourage conversions to Christianity. Laws were passed banning Christians from keeping Hindus in their employ, and the public worship of Hindu Gods was deemed unlawful. The Inquisition was established to punish the relapsed New Christians, but were suspected of practicing their ancestral religion in secret. It prosecuted non-converts who broke prohibitions against the observance of Hindu or Muslim rites, or interfered with Portuguese attempts to convert non-Christians to Catholicism. Thousands of Saraswat Brahmin families fled to interior Maharashtra and coastal Karnataka. Many families fled by ships to the southern ports from Honavar to Kozhikode. Many settled down at these ports, which already contained Saraswat traders and spread into the interior. Others went south to settle in Karwar and South Kanara. The last of those families, landed in Calicut, Kerala around the middle of 16th century but were driven out by the Zamorin rulers; so they went south to Cochin and Travancore.

## GSBs in Karnataka

GSBs first came to Karnataka in the early 14th century, when the region was ruled by Jain Bhairarasa Odeyars. The rulers welcomed the Brahmins and gifted them land to continue their traditional profession as farmers. Many families settled down in smaller towns and villages in Shimoga, South and North Kanara Districts. Being highly literate, GSBs soon settled in to build several remarkable enterprises, especially in banking. Among the pioneers in setting up banking institutions in Mangalore were Ammembal Subba Rao Pai, a Gowd Saraswat Brahmin, who started the Canara Bank in 1906. Another bank, Syndicate Bank in 1925 was founded by T. M. A. Pai, Upendra Pai and Vaman Kudva from Udupi in Karnataka. T. M. A. Pai was a doctor, educationist, banker and philanthropist, most well known for building the university town of Manipal, Karnataka, India. He was first to start a private, self-financing medical college offering MBBS in India. Pai established the Kasturba Medical College, Manipal in 1953 and Manipal Institute of Technology in 1957, which was followed by a string of other education institutions including Kasturba Medical College, Mangalore, Manipal College of Dental Sciences and Manipal College of Pharmaceutical Sciences.

## GSBs in Kerala

The migration of GSBs to Kerala were mainly in two phases; in the 13th century and subsequently in the 16th century (1560 AD).

There is some evidence that a few members of the GSB community had settled in Cochin as early as the 13th century A.D. They created a community called "Konkanastha Mahajanam" and later came to be known as Konkanis. The Raja of cochin gave them his protection. There still remains a place in Cochin called Sashty Parambu Ln to commemorate the fact that the Saraswats of Cochin originally belonged to Sasasti (Salcette). In search of trading opportunities, some moved along the coast and settled in places like Alleppey, Purakkad and Kayamkulam.

The local Brahmins did not recognize Saraswats as Brahmins and were not allowed inside the Kerala temples. This was mainly because many Saraswats were fish eating and some of them came to Kerala by sea. In those days, the Brahmins considered crossing the sea inauspicious. The GSBs wanted to establish their own temples and started worshipping their Kuladevatas in their homes and work settlements. The Kerala GSBs also gave up fish eating to earn their status as Brahmins among the locals.

Around 1791 AD, a new Raja of Cochin ascended the throne, he was known as Sakthan Thampuran. He wanted the wealth amassed by the Konkanis and their temples. The persecuted Konkanis then fled to Thuravoor and Alleppey in the Travancore state and presented their grievances to the Raja of Travancore. Raja of Travancore allowed them to stay there and prosper. Apart from Kochi, Thuravoor and Allapuzzha, there is a significant GSB population in Chertala, North Parur, Varapuzha, Cherai, Vypeen, Tripunithura, Kottayam and Ettumanoor.

# Gowd Saraswat Brahmin Cuisine

Many Saraswat Brahmins are pesco-vegetarians. This is the practice of following a diet that is vegetarian but includes fish or other seafood, but not the flesh of other animals. The inclusion of fish in the diet is not looked upon as non vegetarian. Legend has it that when the Saraswati River dried up, the Saraswats who could not farm, were permitted to eat sea food/fish. The fish were euphemistically called Sea Vegetable. Oysters for example are called 'samudra phalam' meaning sea fruit. The GSBs in Karnataka are usually pesco-vegetarians but GSBs in Kerala are usually vegetarians.

The cuisine revolves around local vegetables, lentils, coconut and rice. GSBs are supposed to be crazy about leafy green vegetables. There is a joke that GSBs could eat any and every leaf on plants and trees! Even though coconut is mixed with greens, GSBs also have very simple, healthy ways to put together a tasty meal with just seasoning of mustard seeds, curry leaves, salt and chillies. Importance is given to balance the meal with different tastes and yet have various digestive elements, including ingredients like gingers, yogurt/curd etc. Tamarind is the main souring agent. Sometimes a special variety of gambodge or Malabar tamarind that is called dharbe sol is used. Carambola, karmbala or star fruit is also a popular souring agent. In Kerala GSBs, recipes typically do not contain onion or garlic, making their cuisine similar to Jains. Karnataka GSBs do use them often.

Asafoetida is another crucial spice in a GSB home. A pinch is must in most lentils and root vegetable curries. The smell of asafoetida might be strong and unpleasant but in cooking it mellows out and produces a flavor similar to onion and garlic.

If one aims to list down the spices used in GSB cuisine, it is limited to mustard seeds, cumin seeds, fenugreek seeds, coriander seeds, curry leaves, cardamom, turmeric powder, red chillies, red chilli powder, green chillies, tamarind and asafoetida. Jaggery is most popular sweeter which not only gives sweetness but texture and color to dishes too.

Teppal is an ingredient commonly used by the GSB families in Karnataka. This is a fruit of the plant grown in Karnataka and Maharashtra which is a species similar to Tirphal (Zanthoxylum rhetsa) and Szechuan pepper (Zanthoxylum piperitum). It looks like big size black pepper berries. This bears fruits during monsoons. During the season, fresh fruits are used while in off-season the seeds are discarded and only the outer layer of the fruit is dried and used in most of the preparations. Teppal is a good cure for dysentery and has many medicinal uses. Mostly used in fish preparation and vegetarian dishes using coconut masala. It has a strong woody aroma. At the time of eating the curry, the Teppal in the curry is not consumed and is discarded. These are slightly crushed in one table spoon of water and added to the gravy while boiling.

Garlic is another spice which is widely used by GSB from Karnataka in their curries. Its usually avoided by GSBs from Kerala yet widely popular in Karnataka GSB. Garlic has a characteristic pungent, spicy flavor that mellows and sweetens considerably with cooking. Garlic has been used medicinally for many years for treating bites, tumors, ulcers, snakebite, wounds, headaches, heart diseases, cancer, pimples, measles and many more. It also prevents infections such as the common cold, cough because of its Anti-bacterial, Anti-fungal and Anti-viral property.

Kokum is yet another spice commonly used by GSBs in Karnataka. Also called Birinda Salle, kokum is used in Kadi preparation. Kadi is made as a thin curry or a watery drink using kokum, coconut milk, asafoetida, chillies and cilantro leaves.  It is known for its digestive properties. It is quite popular in the entire Konkan region.

A typical Breakfast in a GSB home may have included of Undi(rice dumpling), polo (dosa/rice crepe), along with tambali(chutney) and or Sambhar. Shevaiyn phann (thin rice noodles with savory seasoning) or Phow (flattened rice - poha), Goda Phow (with sweet jaggery) or Meet Miryasange Phow (savory with salt and chillies) would be other breakfast specialties.

Lunch and dinner would commonly have Dali Toi (lentil soup) and sheeth (rice). A typical lunch would have Sheeth (rice), Hoomann (spicy curry), ukari ( stir-fry), ghassi ( spicy coconut gravy), nonche ( salt pickled vegetable), Papodd or appol(crisp), and Toi (thin lentil soup) or Kadhi ( thin yogurt curry). Kadhi is made to serve the dual purpose of Mukhashuddhhi (mouth purification, perhaps after all the relatively spicy stuff) and jeervonn (digestive Kadhis include asafoetida, Vomvom, Jeera, fennel seed). Last the godsaniche(sweets), typically doodah payas (milky rice pudding).

# Gowd Saraswat Brahmin Festivals

Most of the Hindu festivals are followed by GSB community but there are a few which are very special to the community. A festival is commonly known as 'parab'. Some traditions are followed for the festivals and some specific dishes are prepared to celebrate those special festivals with a feast called as 'parbe jevan'.

**1.      Samsar Padvo**

Samsar Padvo which is the first day of Chaitra is celebrated as the New Year Day of GSB's. Ugadi and Gudi padva is also celebrated on the same day.

Delicacy prepared on this day is Madagane, 'hittu' using jackfruit leaves and Kele ambatt using jaggery & banana.

**2.      Nagar Panchami**

Celebrated on the 5th day of the bright fortnight in the month of Shravan. Milk is offered to Naga idols with aarthi and prayer to Nagas. Is also celebrated as the victory day of Krishna over the Kaliya snake.

Delicacies prepared on this day are Haldi-Panna Patholi. Panchakadai and Cheppa-Kheeri.

**3.      Sutta-Punav**

On this Shravan full moon day, GSB men change the sacred thread or 'janevu'.

Delicacies prepared on this day are Khotto/ Hitu, Val-Val and Soyi-Bagil Ghessi

**4.      Ganesh Chathurthi**

Festival of Lord Ganesha, Pooja is performed by GSB Men.

Some of the delicacies prepared on this day are Patharodo, Panchakadai and Modak.

**5.      Diwali**

Falls on the 1st day of Karthik month.

Diwali is a very important festival for Konkanis. Family wakes up early in the morning before sun rise. After having scalp massaged with coconut oil, all the family members take bath and wear new clothes. This bath after applying oil on the scalp is the main ritual of the Diwali day. Lighting lamps and bursting fire-crackers are also performed. There is another interesting ritual performed by the eldest woman, daughter-in-law or the lady of the house to remove all bad omen from the house and family members. The lady of the house prepares 5 or 7 deepams/lamp made with rice flour dough, Haldi/turmeric powder and Kum-Kumand/vermillion. The deepams/lamp are filled with oil and a wick is placed in them. Then they are kept in a row on a plate and lit up. A few small balls are also made using the same materials. The lady of the house does the aarti three times, for all family members together. Then, she will take one small ball in her hand and make two rounds - one clockwise and the other anti-clockwise, in front of each family member. She will keep the ball back on the plate and sprinkle a few drops of water on the feet of the family member. This is repeated for everyone in the family. This is supposed to remove the bad-omen. She then carries the plate out-side and throws the contents aside.

The Naivedyam/sacrament called 'Satta-Phovu' prepared with poha/aval/Beaten rice, jaggery/brown sugar, roasted Til/Sesame seed, Bengal gram, green gram and coconut. The must included dishes for Diwali feast are Khotto, Dud-Pak, 'Kuvale-Kachil Ambat, Phodis and Ershale.

## 6.    Thulsi Pooja

Tulsi Pooja is done on the 12th day of Karthik month which usually falls in October/ November. The ritual is performed by the Bhat-Mam/priest or by the eldest man, father or head of the family. This ritual is to conduct the marriage between Lord Vishnu and Tulsi who is believed to be the incarnation of Vrinda, a demi-god mentioned in the Hindu scriptures. On that day of puja, Tulsi-Katte is well decorated with Mango leaves, sugarcane is buried in it and avale (Goosberry) and tamarind branches are put on it. After this Tulsi Poojan (Vivah) usually the wedding season starts in GSB Community.

Godu-Povu is prepared as Naivedyam. Soornali is prepared as a special dish on this day.

# Breakfast

# Undi

## Steamed rice dumpling

Undi, the steamed rice balls are usually eaten with garlic chutney as breakfast or snack.

# Undi – Steamed rice dumpling

**Time**- 30 minutes

**Serves** 10-12 balls

## Ingredients

Cracked raw rice/Rice rava - 1 cup
Grated coconut – ½ cup
Red chillies – 1-2 to taste – finely chopped
White lentil/Urad dal – 1 teaspoon
Mustard seeds – 1 teaspoon
Fenugreek Seeds- ¼ teaspoon
Oil - 1 tablespoons
Salt - to taste

## Method

Heat the oil in a pan.

Add mustard seeds, fenugreek seeds, urad dal and chopped red chillies to the heated oil.

When the ingredients start popping, add rava and fry for 2-3 minutes.

Add salt, grated coconut and 3 cups boiling water. Keep on stirring the ingredients. You need to stir continuously while pouring the boiled water so that the paste does not form lumps.

Keep heat to low and continue stirring until paste is completely cooked.

Let it cool, until it is easy to handle with hands. Form small balls with a hole in the center.

Line up the balls in a pan in a steamer/ cooker or Pedavan. Steam the balls for 15 minutes. Serve hot with Garlic Chutney or any other kind of Chutney.

## TIPS

1. If you are using raw rice instead of rice rava, soak the raw rice for 3 hours. Ground the soaked rice coarsely with a cup of grated coconut. Add 3 cups of water and make a thin batter. In a pan heat oil, season with mustard seeds, fenugreek seeds, urad dal and red chillies. While this is spluttering, slowly pour the batter into the phannu or seasoning while constantly stirring, until it is fully cooked and it becomes semi-solid form. Let it cool. Make balls and steam as the procedure mentioned above.
2. One may add more grated coconut that enhances the coconut taste of Undi.
3. Undi is also eaten with warm jaggery syrup flavoured with cardamom. The other popular accompaniment is garlic chutney.
4. Do not use more fenugreek seeds than above mentioned in ingredients; excessive fenugreek seeds will give a tinge of bitterness to this dish

# Surnali

## Sweet rice pancake

Surnali is also called methi polo and is popular in the entire Konkan belt. Surnali is the special breakfast in GSB homes during Tulasi puja day.

# Surnali – Sweet rice pancake

**Time**- 45 minutes, 4 hours for soaking and 8 hours for fermentation

**Serves** 10-12 pancakes

**Ingredients**

Raw rice - 2 cups
Grated coconut - 2 cups
Sour buttermilk or Curd/Yogurt - 1 cup.
Beaten rice/Poha – ½ cup
Jaggery - 1 ½ cups to taste
Fenugreek Seeds- ¼ teaspoon
Cooking Soda – ¼ teaspoon
Turmeric Powder – ¼ teaspoon
Salt – a pinch
Clarified butter/Ghee – 2 tablespoon

**Method**

Soak Rice and fenugreek seeds for 4 hours.

Soak Poha for 5 minutes.

Grind the soaked ingredients together with grated coconut and buttermilk to make a fine batter. Add jaggery, turmeric powder and a pinch of salt. Blend it well. Final batter must be thick but pourable. If it is too thick, adjust the consistency of the batter by adding water or buttermilk. Be careful not to turn the batter thin.

Leave this to ferment for 8 hours.

After fermentation, beat it until fluffy, add cooking soda and mix well.

Heat a flat pan/tawa. Smear a little ghee/clarified butter on the surface. Pour a ladle of the batter. Do not spread like usual dosa, instead turn the pan around in a circular motion so that batter spreads by itself into a circular shape. Close it with a lid. Cook it on low flame for a minute or less till it is roasted well and one sees pores on the Soornali. No flipping should be done. The Soonali is fried only on one side.

Serve Soornali hot with homemade butter.

<u>TIPS</u>

1. The softness of Soornali depends on quantity of grated coconut.

2. The same batter without jaggery, made into a pancake, is called Cheppi soornali. Cheppi means unsweetened in Konkani. Cheppi Soornali can be eaten with Yam pickle/Soorna Nonche or any other kind of pickle, chutney or curry.

3. This dish though sweet, is especially healthy due to fermentation. Fermentation increases the bioavailability of nutrients like minerals present in food, improves gut health and helps breakdown of anti-nutrients.

# Hittu

## Dumpling steamed in leaf basket

Hittu or Khotto - a typical konkani breakfast prepared during festivals, by using idli batter and steamed in Jackfruit leaf baskets. Jackfruit leaf baskets are prepared using 4 leaves pinned with toothpicks to form a basket. The basket is called Khotto and dumpling known as Hittu in the Kochi side households. Mangalore GSBs call the dumpling as Khotto. You could use any medium sized leaves or even banana leaves, if you don't have jackfruit leaves. Dip the banana leaf pieces in hot water for a few minutes to make it malleable before you make the basket molds or make a cylindrical roll. Tie one end with a string. Fill in the batter and tie the other end too before steaming.

# Hittu – Dumpling steamed in leaf basket

**Time**- 45 minutes, 4 hours for soaking and overnight fermentation

**Serves** 10 – 12 dumplings

**Ingredients**

Urad Dal/ Black Gram lentil - 2 cup

Rice rava - 4 cups

Jack-Fruit Leaves - 44 to 48 leaves

Tooth picks - 50

Salt - to taste

**Method**

Soak the dal in water for about 4 hours.

Grind dal/lentil in grinder or food processor. Adding water little by little, only as needed to grind. Grind till the lentil batter is fluffy. Wash rice rava and drain it completely. Add this into the batter and add salt according to taste. Mix well.

Keep aside to ferment overnight.

Make the baskets with the jackfruit leaves.

Once the fermentation is done (about 8 to 10 hours) mix the batter well. Ladle into the Jackfruit leaf baskets till the basket is little more than half full. These will fluff up while steaming. Steam these baskets in a steamer/pressure cooker or Pedawan for about 25 to 30 minutes. Once cooled, take the hittu out of the leaves by unpinning the toothpicks or tearing the leaves off. Try keep the basket like shape of Hittu intact. Serve with Chutney or Sambar.

<u>TIPS</u>

1. To add flavour to hittu, one may add finely chopped ginger and green chillies into the batter before steaming the hittu.

2. The hittu makes a very healthy breakfast. The combination of rice and lentils makes it a complete dish as it has all the essential amino acids, fiber along with energy of carbohydrates but low calories. This is important for individuals on a vegetarian diet for whom lentils are main source of proteins.

3. This dish is especially healthy due to fermentation. Fermentation increases the bioavailability of nutrients like minerals present in food, improves gut health and helps breakdown of anti-nutrients.

# Adsara polo

## Tender coconut crepe

Adsara polo is popular across the Konkan belt. It is similar to Neer Dosa. Neer Dosa is made with unfermented rice batter where as Adsara polo has tender coconut added to the batter. It is also known as soyi polo or paan polo

# Adsara Polo – Tender coconut crepe

**Time**- 30 Minutes and overnight soaking

**Serves** 10-12 pancakes

**Ingredients**

Raw rice - 2 cup

Grated tender coconut – 1 ½ cups

Water - 6 cups

Salt - to taste

**Method**

Soak the rice overnight.

Post soaking, wash the rice and grind with coconut and water just enough to blend. It should become a smooth pourable batter.

Add water to make the batter slightly thinner than the normal dosa batter.

Add salt to taste.

Prepare dosas. Since the consistency of the batter is thin, one may pour one big ladle of batter in the center of the pan and turn the pan itself to give the batter a round shape.

Cover the dosa with a lid on and cook for some time. This dosa need to be cooked one side only. If the Dosa is sticking to the Pan, one may apply oil on the pan before pouring the batter.

Serve hot polo with dali thoy or sugar & ghee or goda pankh i.e. jaggery syrup or chutney.

## TIPS

1. If coconut water is available, one may add one cup of coconut water by replacing one-cup water in the ingredients. This will make the Soyi Polo soft and also give a better taste.
2. Also called Soyi Polo- Soyi in Konkani means grated coconut. This polo is usually made with tender coconut. However, this could be made with regular coconut also.
3. Rice crepe or dosa in Konkani is called polo. Polo is usually made fluffy soft and not thin and crisp like typical dosa
4. The coconut and rice as ingredients makes it quite light and healthy breakfast.

# Mushti polo

## Rice pancake

Mushti in Konkani means - a fist-full. In this recipe all ingredients (except rice) are measured in a mushti (or fist-full)

# Mushti polo – Rice pancake

**Time**- 25 Minutes, 5 hours for soaking and 8 hours for fermentation

**Serves** – 8-10 pancakes

**Ingredients**

Raw rice - 1 cup

White lentil/Urad dal – 1 fist-full or ¼ cup

Fenugreek seeds/methi- ½ teaspoon

Grated coconut – 2 fist-full or ½ cup

White beaten rice or Poha – 1 fist-full or ¼ cup

Clarified butter/ghee – 2 tablespoons

Finely chopped coriander leaves/Kotambari – 1 cup

Salt - To Taste

**Method**

Wash and soak together, raw rice, urad dal and fenugreek seeds/methi for 5 hours.

Mix the grated coconut and poha with soaked rice, dal and methi; grind to a smooth batter.

Add salt to taste.

Keep the batter to ferment for 8 hours.

Heat a flat pan/tawa and pour a ladle of batter. Spread it lightly, not spreading too much, as this polo is expected to be thick, almost like a pancake and not thin like crepe.

Sprinkle half-teaspoon ghee on top; cover and cook for a minute on medium flame. Do not flip over.

Serve hot Mushti Polo with Kotamberi/Coriander leaves chutney or coconut chutney.

TIPS
1. Combination of rice and lentils in ingredients and fermentation process makes the mushti polo a very healthy breakfast. You can add wheat bran or oat bran in the batter to increase the amount of fiber in the polo/pancakes and make them even healthier dish.
2. Rice pancake or dosa in Konkani is called polo. Polo is usually made fluffy soft, more like pancake, not thin and crisp like dosa or crepe.
3. This dish is especially healthy due to fermentation. Fermentation increases the bioavailability of nutrients like minerals present in food, improves gut health and helps breakdown of anti-nutrients.

# Doddagu

## Semolina pancake

A thick dosa made of lentil and semolina.

# Doddagu – Semolina pancake

**Time-**

5 hours to soak, overnight to ferment and 30 minutes to make pancake

**Serves**

8-10 pancakes

**Ingredients**

Urad Dal/White lentils – 2 cups

Fine Sooji/Rava/Semolina – 2 cups

Ginger – 1-inch piece

Green Chillies – 1 to 2 to taste

Onion (optional) – ¼ piece

Curry leaves – 10-12 leaves

Mustard seeds– ½ Teaspoon

Salt to taste

Oil – 1 Teaspoon for seasoning

Oil – For frying pancakes

**Method**

Wash and soak Urad Dal/White lentils for 5 hours; strain the excess water and grind the lentils to a fluffy fine paste using least amount of water.

Add Sooji/Semolina and mix well with the spoon. You may add some water to bring the paste to the right consistency; the batter should be thick but of dropping consistency.

Keep this aside for fermentation overnight or at the least 8 hours.

Add salt to the fermented batter.

Heat teaspoon of oil in a small pan, add the mustard seeds and let it splutter. Add finely chopped ginger, onion (optional) and green chillies and fry them for a few seconds. Add the curry leaves. Remove from fire and add this seasoning into the fermented batter and mix well.

The batter is now ready to prepare Doddagu.

Heat a tawa/frying pan on medium flame. Pour a ladle of batter and spread it on the tawa. Do not spread much. Sprinkle some oil on the top of the pancake and close it with a lid. After a minute open the lid and if it is cooked, turn over the Doddagu. Once both sides of Doddagu are slightly golden brown, transfer the Doddagu in a plate.

Doddagu is ready to be served with Chutney or Sambar.

<u>TIPS</u>
1. While serving you may sprinkle some grated coconut on top of the Doddagu.
2. In place of Sooji /semolina, one may use red matta or parboiled rice 1 ½ Cups and ½ cup white rice mixture
3. This dish is especially healthy due to fermentation. Fermentation increases the bioavailability of nutrients like minerals present in food, improves gut health and helps breakdown of anti-nutrients.

# Udada appo

## Fried lentil dumpling

Udada Appo is like kara paniyaram made in South India except that udada appo does not have seasoning of onions or shallots but ginger, chillies and curry leaves.

# Udada Appo – Fried lentil dumpling

**Prep Time**- 20 minutes, 5 hours to soak and overnight to ferment

**Serves** – 20-24 dumplings

**Ingredients**

White lentil/Urad Dal - 1 cup
Raw rice - 2 cups
Oil – 4 tablespoons
Salt - To taste

For seasoning -
 Ginger - 1 inch
Green chillies – 1-2 taste
Curry leaves - 10-12

**Method**

Soak the dal and rice, separately, for 5 hours.

Grind the soaked urad dal and rice, separately, in a grinder to fine pastes. Mix both the pastes to make a thick batter. Leave this batter for overnight fermentation.

Finely chop the seasoning ingredients and add to the batter. Add salt to taste. Beat the batter thoroughly so that it fluffs up a little bit.

One needs to use special pan called Paniyarakkal or Appo pan. It looks like as shown in picture on the side. Heat the appo pan, grease with oil and fill the depressions, a little more than half, with batter. Sprinkle some oil over it and close the lid. Let it cook for five minutes on low flame. Open the lid, turn the Appo's over to the other side and roast them for 2 minutes or until they become crisp and golden. Serve hot with any kind of chutneys.

## TIPS

1. Instead of 2 cups of raw rice, using 1 cup boiled rice with 1 cup raw rice will make the softer appos.
2. Adding a pinch of cooking soda will make the Appos softer too.
3. Instead of using 1 cup urad dal; one may use ½ cup urad dal and ½ chana dal to give the recipe a variation.
4. Another variation to make instant appo is making these with rava/semolina and curds instead of rice and lentils. Mix rava with thick curd to make a thick batter. Use this batter to make the appo using same method as above.
5. Consistence of batter should be like Idli batter.
6. This dish is healthy due to good combination of carbohydrates and proteins in rice and lentils. Fermentation makes it even healthier. Fermentation increases the bioavailability of nutrients like minerals present in food, improves gut health and helps breakdown of anti-nutrients.

# Moodo

## Rice dumpling

Moodo is very similar to khotto, since the basic batter is the idli batter. There are especially made during Konkani festivals of Navratri and Suttan-punnav, etc.

Leaf mold or containers are made with Screw pine/Kedige leaves. Leaves are washed and cleaned. Roll the leaves in a cylindrical shape and fix them in shape using toothpicks. Vegetable vendors sell such leaf molds during festival times in areas around Mangalore and many other places. You could try make it with banana leaves if you are unable to get these Kedige leaf molds. Dip the banana leaf pieces in hot water for a few minutes to make it malleable before you make the cylindrical molds.

# Moodo – Rice dumpling

**Time**

60 minutes cooking, 4 hours for soaking and 8 hours for fermentation

**Serves**

4-5 cylindrical dumplings

**Ingredients**

Urad Dal/white lentils – ½ cup
Rice - 1 cup
Salt to taste
Screw Pine/Kedige leaf
Molds/containers – 5

**Method**

Soak urad dal/white lentils and rice separately for 4 hours.

Grind urad dal/white lentils in a grinder, adding a little water at a time until it rises to 3 times volume you started with. Consistency of the ground urad dal/white lentils must be fluffy and light, not runny. Pour the ground urad dal/white lentils in a bowl.

Now grind the rice coarsely using very little water.

Mix the rice batter with the urad dal/white lentils batter and leave it for fermentation for 8 hours.

Add salt to the batter and mix well. The consistency of the batter should be thicker than the usual idli batter.

Boil 500ml water in the pressure cooker. Fill the moodo leaf container 2/3rd with batter. This will increase in volume as it steams. Steam the moodos in the pressure cooker on medium flame without using the weight for about an hour. Turn off the heat and let it cool down. Once it is completely cooled, unwrap the steamed moodo by removing the toothpicks and sliding off the leaf so that moodo does not break.

Serve hot with Sambar and Coconut Chutney.

## TIPS

1. To make the moodos soft, the lentil batter should be fluffy and light. Grind the lentil paste for longer period of time. You might have to rest your food processor in between the grinding.

2. You may steam the Moodo in a steamer or Idli Pedavan.

3. You can use Sooji/Semolina instead of rice. In this case, you need to steam Sooji in the pressure cooker for 10 minutes. Let it cool down to room temperature before adding this into the urad dal/white lentils batter.

4. This dish is healthy due to good combination of carbohydrates and proteins in rice and lentils. Fermentation makes it even healthier. Fermentation increases the bioavailability of nutrients like minerals present in food, improves gut health and helps breakdown of anti-nutrients.

# Phanna polo

## Crepe with seasoning

An instant dosa or crepe that can be prepared quickly without usual elaborate soaking, grinding and fermentation for dosa.

# Phanna polo – Crepe with seasoning

**Time**

30 minutes

**Serves**

6 – 8 crepes

**Ingredients**

Maida or Wheat flour - 2 cups

Green chillies – 2-3 to taste

Water for preparing the batter

Grated coconut – ½ cup

For Seasoning -

Mustard Seeds – ¾ teaspoon

Curry Leaves – 5-6

Oil – 2 tablespoons

**Method**

Grind the green chillies with grated coconut and salt in a food processor.

Add coconut paste and water to flour to make a thick batter. Mix well avoiding any lumps, until you get a smooth and thick consistency. Keep this aside.

Heat a teaspoon of oil in a frying pan. Season with mustard seeds and once this splutters, add curry leaves. Pour this seasoning into the batter and mix well. Add salt to taste.

Pour a ladle of seasoned dosa batter on a preheated pan seasoned with a few drops of oil and spread as thin as you like. Use a non-stick pan to make the crepe crisp without using much oil.

Fry till crispy and golden on both sides.

Serve with Chutney Podi (Pola Pitti) or pickle.

<u>TIPS</u>
1. Use cast-iron pan for frying for a crispy dosa.
2. If the crepe/dosa is sticky and not coming out of the pan easily, let the dosa cook in medium flame for a slightly longer time.
3. You can make this instant dosa without grated coconut, with plain wheat flour. It is called Gova polo or wheat dosa.
4. Add wheat or oats bran or gram flour/besan to the batter to make this crepe nutritious and fiber rich.

## Snacks

# Goli Bajje

## Flour fritters

This is also called Mangalore Bajji or Bonda

# Goli bajje – Flour fritters

**Time -** 30 minutes and 1 hour for batter to ferment

**Serves**

18-20 fritters

**Ingredients**

Maida/All purpose flour – 2 cups
Besan/chickpea-gram flour – ½ cup
Butter Milk (or thick curd/yogurt) ½ cup
Water – ½ cup
Sugar – 2 teaspoons
Soda Bi-Carb – 1 teaspoon
Ginger – ½ inch piece chopped
Green Chillies – 4 – 5 finely chopped
Finely chopped coconut pieces – 1 teaspoon
Curry leaves – 4 -5 leaves finely chopped
Coriander leaves – 1 teaspoon finely chopped

**Method**

Beat buttermilk or thick curd or yogurt with water till fluffy. Add sugar, salt and soda bi-carb and mix well. Add flour and Besan/chickpea flour. Mix well and ensure there are no lumps.

Then add all the other ingredients and make it into a smooth batter. Make sure that the batter is not watery. It should be Idli batter consistency. Leave aside the batter for an hour.

Heat oil till smoking then reduce heat to medium. Take a spoon full of batter and drop it in oil. Flip around and let the fritters fry on both sides. Ensure the oil is not too hot that it doesn't cook inside but browns outside too fast. It shouldn't be less hot either else it will absorb too much oil. When they are golden brown, remove them from oil. Goli baje is ready to serve.

Serve Goli baje with thick coconut chutney.

<u>TIPS</u>

1. You can use ¼ cup of rice flour along-with 1 ¾ cup of maida/flour instead of 2 cups maida/flour. This little amount of rice flour will help make the bajje crispier.
2. You may add a pinch of hing/Asafoetida and 6-7 kernels crushed black pepper instead of the 4 – 5 green chillies.
3. This is a good snack to eat with tea or coffee but in moderation.

# Biscoot rotti

## Stuffed fritters

Biscoot rotti or Mangalore kachori is a popular snack in GSB homes especially when guests come home.

# Biscoot rotti – Stuffed fritters

**Time**
60 Minutes
**Serves**
10-12 fritters
**Ingredients**
For the **dough**
Maida/Flour – 2 cups
Wheat flour – 1 cup
Salt – a pinch.
Sugar – a pinch
Hot oil – 2 – 3 tablespoons
Haldi/Turmeric powder – a pinch.
Water – to make a soft dough
For the **filling**
Grated coconut – ½ cup
Bombay sooji/Semolina– ¾ cup
Red chilly powder – 1 teaspoon
Green chillies – 2 chopped
Mustard seeds – 1 teaspoon
Urad dal/white lentil – 1 teaspoon
Curry leaves – 10 leaves chopped
Hing/Asafoetida – ¼ teaspoon
Coriander leaves – 10 leaves
chopped
Sugar – a pinch
Ginger – 1-inch piece finely
chopped
Besan/chickpea flour – 2
tablespoons (optional)
Jeera/cumin & Coriander Seeds –
mixed – 1 teaspoon (optional)
Oil – for deep frying

**Method**
For the filling-

Heat teaspoon oil in a small pan. Add mustard seeds. Once the seeds splutter, add grated ginger, finely chopped green chillies, curry leaves, urad dal, and crushed jeera/cumin-coriander seeds mixture, red chilly powder and hing/Asafoetida. Sauté them for a minute; add besan/chickpea flour into it and fry for about five minutes till you get a nice aroma of fried chickpea flour. Now add sooji/semolina and grated coconut and roast it for another two minute. Turn off the heat. Add chopped coriander leaves, haldi/turmeric powder, sugar and salt. Mix well. This mixture is ready for filling. Keep this aside.

For the dough-

Mix well maida/flour, wheat flour, salt and sugar. Pour 2-tablespoon hot oil into it. With the help of water knead it into a stiff (semi-soft) dough. Cover the dough with a damp cloth and keep it aside for 15 minutes.

Make small balls from the dough and roll them into puris (3 – 4-inch diameter discs).

Place a tablespoon of the filling in the center of the puri and cover-up fully by gathering-up the edges and sealing all the sides. Roll it again gently into a puri / disc while applying a bit of dry flour. Be careful not to have the filling come out of the puri while rolling.

Repeat the procedure with all the puris.

Deep-fry them in medium hot oil. With the help of a ladle press the center of the puri to puff it up. Fry both the sides till golden brown.

Serve bisoot rotti hot with tea or coffee.

## TIPS

1. The heat of the Oil must be medium while frying. This makes Rotti's with crispy outer crust.
2. Frequent pressing of the Puri center with ladle makes the Rotti puff-up.
3. This is a good snack to eat with tea or coffee but in moderation.

# Cabbageja undi

## Cabbage dumpling

Cabbage undi is also known as cabbage mudho

# Cabbageja undi – Cabbage dumpling

**Time**

60 Minutes cooking and 3 hours soaking

**Serves**

10-12 dumplings

**Ingredients**

Cabbage – 250 - 300 grams

Onion - 2 (optional)

Yellow lentil/Tur dal – ¼ Cup

Raw rice – ¾ Cup

Grated coconut - 1 Cup

Red chillies – 3-5 to taste

Tamarind - as the same size of a marble.

Asafoetida/Hing - 1 Teaspoon.

Salt to taste.

**Method**

Soak the rice and tur dal/yellow lentils together for 3 hours.

Roast red chillies in a few drops of oil. Grind grated coconut, red chillies, tamarind and Asafoetida/hing to a smooth paste. Add soaked dal, rice mixture and salt into this paste and grind again, till you get a coarse thick paste. Use as little water as possible to grind.

Chop cabbage and onions finely. Add chopped cabbage and optionally onion into the paste. The batter should be thicker than the idli batter.

Make 2-inch diameter balls or put a tablespoon full of batter in the idli mold and place in the steamer or idli steamer. You could steam these dumplings in banana leaves. To steam in a banana leaf, place one serving spoon full of batter into each banana leaf piece, fold and steam in a steamer or idli steamer.

Steam for about 30 minutes. Serve hot.

While serving, you may sprinkle half teaspoon of oil on each of the dumpling.

## TIPS

1. You may prepare Mudho/ Undi without adding Tur Dal; in the place of Tur Dal you may use 1 glass boiled rice instead of ¾ glass of raw rice as given in the above recipe.

2. With the same batter, you can use drumstick or methi leaves in the place of Cabbage and Onion.

3. To prepare smooth Mudho / Idli or Undi, you may increase the quantity of Coconut in the recipe.

4. This dish is healthy due to good combination of carbohydrates and proteins in rice and lentils. Cabbage is an excellent source of vitamin C and a very good source of manganese.

# Chettambado

## Cabbage fritters

Ambado is a GSB version of very popular spicy vada of south India. This is usually eaten with rice and dali toy as an accompaniment to a meal.

# Chettambado – Cabbage fritters

**Time**

60 minutes and 2 hours soaking

**Serves**

10-12 fritters

**Ingredients**

Raw rice – ½ cup
Yellow lentil/Tur dal - ½ cup
Onions - 2 medium sized
Cabbage – 200 grams
Red chillies – 4-5 to taste
Grated coconut - 2 tablespoon
Tamarind - ½ lemon size
Salt to taste
Oil for deep frying

**Method**

Wash rice and tur dal; soak them together for 2 hours.

Drain the water and grind the rice-dal mixture with the red chillies, tamarind, grated coconut and salt to a coarse paste without adding any water. Coarsely ground batter with very less or no water will give a nice crunch to the ambado fritter.

Finely chop onions and cabbage and add to the batter. Add salt to taste. Mix well. It should be a thick batter.

Heat up enough oil in a deep frying pan for deep-frying the ambado fritter.

While the oil is heating, roll a handful of batter into lemon sized balls and then slightly flatten them. Once the oil is hot, drop these flattened balls one by one into the pan. Fry until they cook uniformly inside and outside.

Serve hot.

<u>TIPS</u>
1. Do not fry the Ambados on very hot oil on high flame; if so, you may get a crispy Ambado outside and raw inside. So make sure you set the heat on medium.
2. Nice to eat as a crisp along with lunch. Should be eaten in moderation.

# Phodi

## Vegetable fritter

Phodi is a special Konkani fritters made during festivals, especially Ganesh Chaturthi. Phodi can be made with kadgi/tender jackfruit, geev kadgi/breadfruit, Vaigan/eggplant, karathe/bitter gourd, sooran/yam, phagil/teasel gourd, harve kele/raw banana etc.

Phodis are usually served as crisps along with lunch or dinner.

# Phodi – Vegetable fritter

**Prep Time**
30 Minutes
**Serves**
25 – 30 fritters
**Ingredients**
Phagil /teasel gourd – ½ Kgs
Geev-Kadgi – ½ Kgs
(Or 30 pieces of desired Vegetables).
Chilli powder – 2 tablespoons to taste
Hing/Asafoetida – ½ teaspoon
Haldi/turmeric powder – 1 pinch
Thick Tamarind Juice – 2 teaspoon
Salt to taste.
Coriander powder – 2 teaspoon (optional)
Rice flour – ½ cup
Oil – for deep frying

**Method**
Wash & chop the vegetables into large but thin slices. Dry them thoroughly.
Marinate with hing/asafoetida, haldi/turmeric powder, tamarind juice, salt and a tablespoon of chilli powder. Keep aside for 10 minutes. Be careful not to keep the vegetable slices for more than 10 minutes, since the vegetables will start to leave too much water.
Heat the oil and keep ready for frying.
Mix the rice flour with a tablespoon of chilli powder and salt.
Dip the vegetable slice into this seasoned flour till it coats all sides of the slice.
Drop these slices into the hot oil one by one. Turn them from side to side. Remove from oil once they turn golden on all sides.
Drain them of oil using kitchen paper.
Phodis are ready to be served with lunch or dinner.

## TIPS

1. In marinating spices, one may add garlic for flavor.
2. Instead of dry rice powder, one may make a batter out of besan/chonya-pitti/chickpea flour, chilli powder, salt & hing/Asafoetida, and dip the vegetable slices into this wet batter and deep-fry them. This kind of phodi is good to serve with tea or coffee as a snack.
3. One may bake or grill the phodis to cut down the calories from deep-frying and turning them into healthy accompaniment to meals.
4. Should be eaten in moderation.

# Side Dish

## Patharvodo

### Colocasia leaf roll

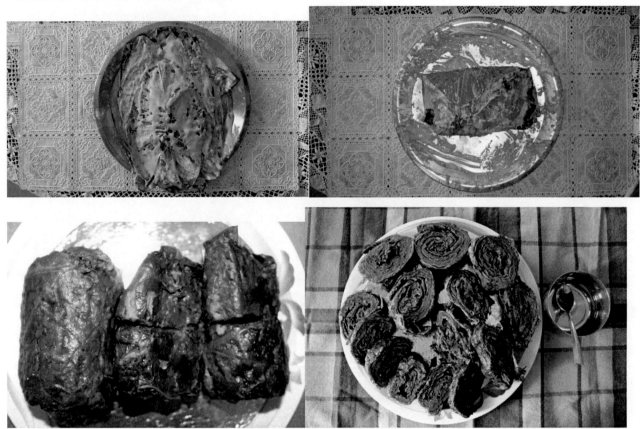

GSBs love all kind of leaves in their cuisine but colocasia leaf dishes have a cult following. There are variety of curries you could make with colocasia leaves but pathorvodo is probably the favorite and most famous. It is made for special occasions when someone visits from afar. Once you realize how simple it is indeed to make, we are sure, you would make it as often as you are able to get these leaves.

# Patharvodo – Colocasia leaf roll

**Time**

120 Minutes and overnight soaking

**Serves**

2 – 3 Persons

**Ingredients**

Tender colocasia leaves– 10-12
For **rice paste** –
Boiled rice – ½ cup
Raw rice – ½ cup
Grated coconut – ½ cup
Tamarind – 1 tablespoon
Asafoetida – 2 pinch
Red chillies – 2 to taste
Turmeric powder – 1 teaspoon
Salt - to taste
For **frying** –
Oil – 2 tablespoon

**Method**

Soak both type of rice in lots of water overnight. Grind rice with all ingredients mentioned for rice paste, using very little water into a paste. Add salt to taste.

Clean the leaves with water and pat them dry with a cloth. Remove veins on the leaves, as much possible without tearing the leaves.

Try stacking the leaves according to their sizes, largest below and smallest on top as you apply the rice paste on them. Ensure the leaf is completely covered with a thin layer of rice paste. Then place next smaller leaf on it. Repeat the rice batter application, till all leaves are exhausted but ensure you do not have more than a dozen in one stack. If you have lots of leaves them make multiple rolls, using the same process of stacking.

Once the leaves have been all layered, roll it up in a cylindrical shape. Push the side edges inside so that, it not a tapering cylinder but flat on both sides. Tie the roll with a clean cotton string.

Steam the roll for an hour and half or more till the needle pricked deep in the roll comes out clean.

Slice the roll into 1 cm circular pieces. You can eat these slices as is with liberal dripping of coconut oil. You could fry them on a pan with a oil till crispy. Serve hot.

<u>TIPS</u>

1. Ensure the colocasia leaves are extremely tender one, else they have tendency to itch in the throat. Mature leaves contain tiny crystals of a substance called calcium oxalate, which makes the throat itch. You can identify mature leaf by bigger veins on the leaf.
2. If you are not sure of their tenderness, soak them in water mixed with some tamarind, for an hour. This can reduce the itching.
3. Ensure the rolls are cooked at the least for an hour. Cooking removes the oxalates which itch the throat
4. Also apply oil on your hand while handling the colocasia leaves so that your hands don't itch.
5. Colocasia leaves are a good source of Vitamin B6 and Phosphorus, and a very good source of Dietary Fibre, Protein, Vitamin A, Vitamin C, Thiamin, Riboflavin, Niacin, Folate, Calcium, Iron, Magnesium, Potassium, Copper and Manganese.

# Vaisambala ukari

## Broad beans stir fry

This is also known as vallasangh ukari.

# Vaisambala ukari – Broad beans stir fry

**Time**

30 Minutes

**Serves**

2-3 bowls

**Ingredients**

Broad beans/Vaisambala – 250 grams
Grated coconut – ¼ cup
Salt - to taste

For seasoning -
Mustard seeds – ¼ teaspoon
Urad dal/white lentil – ¼ teaspoon
Green chillies – 2 to taste
Dry red chillies – 1-2 to taste
Curry leaves – 8-10
Oil – 1 tablespoon

**Method**

De-vein and chop the broad beans into thin slivers.

Heat a tablespoon of oil in a large pan and season with a teaspoon of mustard seeds. As they splutter, add urad dal, dry red chillies and curry leaves. Sauté them for a few seconds.

Add the chopped broad beans/vaisambala to it. Add salt to taste. Sprinkle some water. Stir to mix the ingredients together and cover with a lid. They should be cooked well but hold shape and not become mushy. It might take about 10 minutes. Sprinkle some more water if beans are not cooked. Let it all cook together till they soften and all water has evaporated.

Garnish with grated coconut. Take it off the heat. Serve hot.

**TIPS**

1. Ukari is typical Konkani curry. Usually made by seasoning the ingredients and cooking with little or no water. End product will be totally dry.
2. This is quite a healthy curry with just minimum use of oil.
3. Broad bean is very low in saturated fat, cholesterol and sodium. It is also a good source of dietary fibre, protein, phosphorus, copper and manganese, and a very good source of folate.

# Avnas ambe sassam

## Pineapple mango sweet curry

A coconut based sweet, sour and spicy Konkani mixed fruit dish. This is commonly prepared in summer, the mango season. This is a special dish in menu of a Konkani function such as marriage and upanayanam thread ceremony.

# Avnas ambe sassam – Pineapple mango sweet curry

**Prep Time**

15 - 20 Minutes

**Serves**

4 - 5 bowls

**Ingredients**

Pineapple (peeled & chopped into small pieces) - 1 cup

Mango (peeled & chopped into small pieces) - 1 medium sized

Black seedless grapes - 15

Fresh grated coconut – ¾ cup

Roasted Red Chillies - 2-3 Nos.

Jaggery - 4 tablespoons to taste.

Mustard seeds (dry roasted) - 1 teaspoon.

Salt - ¼ teaspoon to taste.

**Method**

Add all the chopped fruits in a bowl and keep aside.

To prepare the masala, grind grated coconut, roasted red chillies, jaggery, dry roasted mustard seeds and salt into a coarse paste. Add required water to make the paste but the masala should not be watery but paste in consistency.

Transfer this masala into the bowl of the mixed fruits. Mix well.

Avnas Ambe Sassam is ready to be served. Serve chilled or at room temperature.

**TIPS**

1. Jaggery can be substituted with sugar. One could use sugar-free also in case you want to make it without sugar.

2. You may season the sassam with oil, mustard seeds and curry leaves to enhance the flavor.

3. Fruits are sources of many essential nutrients like potassium, dietary fiber, vitamin C, and folate. Mango is rich in pre-biotic dietary fiber, vitamins, minerals, and poly-phenolic flavonoid antioxidant compounds. Coconut is full of vitamins E & C, healthy fat - MCT, electrolytes like potassium, magnesium, manganese, sodium and fiber. This curry made of mixed fruits with coconut is healthy and should be included in daily diet.

# Ambya Umman

## Sweet Mango curry

Ambya umman or ambya ukari is a famous GSB sweet curry, generally made in the summer, the mango season. This curry is prepared with special mangoes known as gointo ambo. This has lots of fibrous pulp. You may also use other type of mangoes which are sweet and sour in taste for this curry.

# Ambya Umman – Sweet Mango curry

**Prep Time**

30 Minutes

**Serves**

6 - 7 bowls

**Ingredients**

Ripe mangoes (sweet & sour) - 8 to 10 preferably small.
Green chillies - 2 Nos. slit.
Jaggery – ½ cup to taste.
Maida/Flour - 2 tablespoon
Salt - 1 pinch
For the seasoning-
Oil - 2 teaspoon
Mustard seeds – ½ teaspoon
Fenugreek seeds/methi – ¼ teaspoon
Urad dal – ¼ teaspoon
Curry leaves - 10
Red chillies - 2 to taste

**Method**

Wash the mangoes and peel off the skin of the mangoes. Keep the peeled mangoes in a bowl and the skin in another bowl.

Add a cup of water to the mango skin and squeeze out the pulpy juice and add to the peeled mangoes. Repeat this till you get all the pulp out of the mango skin. Throw away the skin.

Now add jaggery, green chillies and salt to the mangoes and cook the mangoes on low flame while constantly stirring for about 10 minutes.

Make a thin paste of maida/flour in a cup of water. Add the maida/flour paste into the boiling mangoes while continuing to stir. Boil this mixture well till the sauce thickens. Switch off the flame.

In a pan, heat oil, add mustard seeds and let them splutter. Then, add fenugreek seeds, curry leaves, urad dal and red chillies and fry for a few seconds. Season this to the ambya umman and keep the umman covered.

Ambya umman is ready to serve.

<u>TIPS</u>

1. If you are using big mangoes, you may slice the mangoes and use the slices along with skin. To get all the pulp out of the skin, gentle mash them with the water before squeezing out the pulpy juice.
2. You may add a teaspoon of fresh powdered pepper corn into the seasoning to give the umman a peppery flavour.
3. This can also be eaten chilled.
4. Mango is rich in pre-biotic dietary fibre, vitamins, minerals, and poly-phenolic flavonoid antioxidant compounds.

# Tendle talasani

Ivy gourd stir fry

Tendle talasani is a simple Konkani stir-fry tempered with lots of garlic and chillies.

# Tendle talasani – Ivy gourd stir fry

**Time**

30 Minutes

**Serves**

2 - 3 bowls

**Ingredients**

Tendle/Ivy gourd – 250 grams
Red chillies (long ones) – 4 – 5
Oil – 2 tablespoons
Garlic – 12 – 14 cloves
Salt to taste.

**Method**

Wash tendle/ivy gourds; remove the ends and crush them slightly using a pestle or a heavy ladle. Add salt to these crushed tendle/ivy gourds and keep it aside.

Chop the chillies. Peel the garlic cloves. Crush the garlic cloves also using a pestle or a heavy ladle. In a pan, heat oil, add crushed garlic and fry them till golden brown. Then add chopped red chillies and sauté them too.

Now add crushed tendle/ivy gourds and mix well. Just sprinkle some water and let it cook covered on low flame Stir occasionally. Sprinkle some more water if necessary to cook the gourds. They should be soft but should not lose shape. Once all water has evaporated, sauté them until slightly crisp. Remove from fire.

Tendle Talasni is good to serve with rice, dal and papad.

## TIPS

1. If you like it spicy, increase the number of chillies and also the oil to fry. Tendle tastes great when made spicy.
2. Use only very tender fresh tendle; ripened or stale tendle will not be good for talasani.
3. Ivy gourd has the ability to control blood sugar levels in a natural way. This is because of the liver enzyme in the vegetable that controls the metabolism rate of sugar in the body.

# Gossale ukari

## Ridge gourd stir fry

Gossale ukari is quick to make, takes less than half an hour and a sweet vegetable which makes it a favorite ukari among GSBs.

# Gossale Ukari – Ridge gourd stir fry

**Time**

25 Minutes

**Serves**

4 - 5 bowls

**Ingredients**

Gossale/Ridge gourd – 2 big or
3 medium sized
Oil – 2 teaspoon
Mustard seeds - ¼ teaspoon
Ginger – 1-inch piece
Onion – ¼ piece (optional)
Green chilly – 3
Curry leaves – 8 -10 leaves
Salt to taste.

**Method**

Wash, peel all the ridges of the Gossale/ridge gourd and chop into an inch size pieces. Finely chop ginger, green chillies and curry leaves.

Heat oil in a pan; add mustard seeds and when it crackles, put the chopped ginger, green chillies and curry leaves. Sauté for a minute. Then add the gossale/ridge gourd pieces and salt.

Water is not required for cooking, as gossale contains lot of water in it. Cook with lid-on on a low fire until done. Gossale/ridge gourd pieces should be soft yet not disintegrated.

Gosale ukari is ready to serve with rice and dali toye.

<u>TIPS</u>

1. When you select gossale/ridge gourd, it must be fresh, green and tender.
2. Do not over-cook the Ukari, the gosale should be soft but hold shape.
3. Ridge gourd is extremely healthy vegetable as it is quite low in saturated fats as well as calories and abundant with dietary fiber, vitamin C, riboflavin, zinc, thiamin, iron, as well as magnesium. This is quite recommended for diabetics.

# Padale ukari

## Snake gourd stir fry

Padale or snake gourd is a vegetable commonly found in South India. Padale ukari is a simple recipe that can be prepared in less than half an hour. Snake gourd (also known as potlakaya, chichinda, padwal in Indian languages) is so-called because it looks like a snake, and can grow anywhere from a foot to six feet in length, sometimes curling in on itself if not stretched out with a stone (or other weight) tied to the end while it's growing.

# Padale Ukari – Snake gourd stir fry

**Time**

25 Minutes

**Serves**

4 - 5 Persons

**Ingredients**

Pedale/Snake gourd – 2 big or 3 medium
Oil – 2 teaspoon
Mustard -1/4 teaspoon
Urad dal/white lentil – ½ teaspoon (optional)
Slit green or red chilly – 2-3
Curry leaves – 8 – 10 leaves
Grated coconut – 3 teaspoons
Salt to taste

**Method**

Wash the pedale/snake gourd, scrap the skin off, and cut into thin pieces.

Heat oil in a pan; add mustard seeds and when it crackles, put the urad dal and fry until the dal is light brown in color. Add the slit chillies, curry leaves and add the pedale/snake gourd pieces.

Add salt to taste and stir well.

Sprinkle a few drops of water and cook covered with a lid on, on a low fire. Stir occasionally.

Cook for about 15minutes until it is done. Sprinkle the grated coconut over the ukari and remove it from the fire.

Pedale ukari is ready to serve with rice.

**TIPS**

1. While adding grated coconut, you can mix ¼ teaspoon of haldi/turmeric powder along with the grated coconut and then sprinkle over the ukari. Haldi/turmeric powder not only gives a good color to the ukari, but also has many medicinal values.

2. Snake gourd is a good source of minerals like magnesium, calcium, and phosphorus. Like other gourds such as bottle gourd and ridge gourd, snake gourd is very high in water content and has a cooling effect on the body; hence this summer vegetable that nature provides in such a timely manner helps in handling the summer heat. Because of its high water content, snake gourd is low in calories, fat-free but filling, and great to include in weight-loss diets. Snake gourd also contains a lot of fiber that can help keep your digestive tract healthy. The fiber is also helpful for those with diabetes.

# Kirlele methia sukke

## Sprouted fenugreek seeds stir fry

A very nutritious dish, prepared in Kochi side GSB homes, usually served during special occasion of festivals or weddings.

# Kirlele methia sukke – Sprouted fenugreek seed stir fry

**Time**

2 ½ days for soaking & sprouting, 30 minutes to cook

**Serves**
2-3 bowls
**Ingredients**
Methi/Fenugreek Seeds – 100 grams
Water to soak
Clean cotton cloth to use for keeping the seeds to sprout or germinate

For seasoning
Oil – 1 tablespoon
Mustard seeds – ½ teaspoon.
Urad dal/white lentils– ¼ Teaspoon.
Tamarind – 1 small marble size
Curry leaves – 10-12 leaves
Grated coconut – ½ cup
Red chilly powder – ½ teaspoon to taste
Turmeric powder– ¼ teaspoon
Salt to taste.
Jeera/Cumin (optional) – ¼ teaspoon

**Method**
Wash and soak methi/fenugreek seeds in enough water to immerse them, for 6 hours. Drain and pack it in a clean cotton cloth. Tie it into a bundle and keep aside in a bowl for 2 days to allow the seeds to sprout or germinate. Sprinkle some water occasionally to keep the bundle moist. This will help in accelerating the sprouting/ germination. When methi/fenugreek seeds have sprouted over an inch of sprout, it is ready to cook.

Soak tamarind in a half cup water.

Heat teaspoon of oil in a pan; add mustard seeds and, when they crackle add urad dal, jeera/cumin (optional) and curry leaves.

Add sprouted methi/fenugreek seeds and sprinkle 3 tablespoons of water. Mix all the ingredients well. Cover with a lid and let it cook on medium heat for 10 minutes. Remove the lid; add grated coconut, chilly powder, and turmeric powder, salt, thick tamarind juice. Add salt to taste. Mix well and let the methi cook for another 10 minutes with the lid-on.

When the methi sprouts soften and water dries up, switch off the flame. The sukke is ready to be served with rice.

<u>TIPS</u>
1. Sprouted methi/fenugreek seeds are slightly bitter in taste, but have high nutritional value. It is rich in vitamin C, proteins, fibers, niacin, potassium, iron and alkaloids. Fenugreek contains about 75% soluble fiber that also simulates a feeling of fullness hence fenugreek is a double action solution for weight watchers.
2. It is believed to be one of the best home-remedies in bringing sugar levels down for diabetes.

# Dali toye

## Lentil soup

Dali toye is a very popular Konkani dish which needs no introduction in GSB community. Dali toy is usually served with rice but is also eaten with breakfast dishes khotto/hittu and moode.

# Dali toye – Lentil soup

**Prep Time**

30 Minutes

**Serves**

3 -4 bowls

**Ingredients**

Yellow lentil/Tur Dal - 1 cup
Asafoetida/Hing – ¼ teaspoon
Green Chillies – 2-3 to taste
Salt to taste
Coriander Leaves – a few for garnishing

For Seasoning-
Mustard seeds – ¼ teaspoon
Red Chillies - 2 - 3 to taste
Oil - 2 teaspoon
Curry leaves – 6-8

**Method**

Wash the dal and slit the green chillies in middle. Pressure cook dal along with the green chillies. Churn the cooked dal using a blender or hand churner. Add a little water to get thin soupy consistency. Place the dal back on fire. Add salt and asafoetida/hing. Let it come to boil.

In a deep pan heat teaspoon oil and add mustard seeds, let them splutter. Then add curry leaves and broken red chillies and toss them around. Do not allow the chillies to burn. Add the seasoning to the cooked dal. Take off the heat.

Garnish with coriander leaves and serve hot with rice.

**TIPS**

1. You may add ½ teaspoon turmeric powder while cooking the dal to give the toy a pleasing golden color.

2. You can also add cumin seeds in the seasoning along with mustard seeds to give a variation.

3. Lentils contain the highest amount of protein originating from any plant making them as must have for vegetarians. They are a good source of dietary fiber and also have a low amount of calories. Other nutritious components found are molybdenum, folate, tryptophan, manganese, iron, phosphorous, copper, vitamin B1, and potassium.

# Kele ambat

## Sweet banana curry

A sweet and spicy banana curry prepared in GSB homes, is an excellent accompaniment to a vegetarian feast especially during festival times.

Bananas are naturally sweet and can help curb your sweet tooth if you get that afternoon sugar craving. A 6-inch banana has minimal calories; about one-fourth of the calories you would get from a chocolate candy bar. Additionally, about half of the fibre content in bananas is soluble. Alongside the high levels of potassium and vitamin B6, bananas also have good levels of vitamin C, magnesium and manganese.

# Kele ambat – Sweet banana curry

**Prep Time**

45 Minutes

**Serves**

4 to 5 bowls

**Ingredients**

Half ripe Nendran Banana - 2
Yellow gram lentil/Chana Dal –
150 grams
Jaggery (Gur)/brown sugar –
150 grams
Cashew Nuts – 50 grams
Dry red chillies – 2-3 to taste
Mustard seeds - 1 teaspoon
Cumin Seeds - ¾ teaspoon
Curry leaves – 6-8
Grated coconut – 2 cups
Turmeric Powder – ½ teaspoon
Salt to taste
Clarified butter/ Ghee - 1
Tablespoon

**Method**

Peel and split length-wise the semi-ripe bananas, and cut them into 1½-inch pieces.

Grind the grated coconut and the dry chillies with water to a fine paste.

Cook dal and cashew with water double their volume. Make sure that the dal is not over-cooked, lose shape and become mushy.

In a deep pan, melt the jaggery with half a cup of water on a low flame. Add banana pieces. Boil on medium heat till the banana is cooked. Now add the cooked dal and cashew nuts along with turmeric powder and salt. Add the ground coconut paste also. Add water if needed to get thick curry consistency. Let it boil for a few minutes. Take it off the heat.

In a small pan, heat a tablespoon of ghee, add the mustard seeds. Let them crackle and then add cumin seeds and the curry leaves. Garnish the Kele ambat with this seasoning.

Stir and serve hot.

**TIPS**

1. Do not over-cook the dal and bananas; otherwise the Ambatt will taste like pudding and not curry.

2. In case you are vegan, you may use a teaspoon of oil for seasoning. Ghee gives it a nice festive aroma and flavor but one could use coconut oil to get nice flavor.

3. One may avoid cashew nuts in case of nuts allergy.

4. Ambat made without ghee or cashew nuts and reduced amount of jaggery, reduces the calories of the dish and makes it a healthy sweet curry.

# Bhenda sagle

## Okra curry

Okra/Bhenda is one of the most popular vegetables in all regions of India. GSBs are no different in this aspect. Okra is their favorite too. A dry okra/bhenda curry with coconut, especially for bhenda lovers.

# Bhenda sagle – Okra curry

**Time**

30 Minutes

**Serves**

2-3 bowls

**Ingredients**

Okra/Bhenda - 15 -18
For **paste** -
Grated coconut - 1 cup
Red chillies - 2 - 5 to taste
Tamarind - a small marble size.
Fenugreek seeds/Methi - ¼
teaspoon
Coriander seeds - 2 teaspoon
Water - ½ cup
Salt to taste
For **seasoning** -
Mustard seeds - 1 teaspoon
Curry leaves – 10-12
Oil – 1 ½ teaspoon

**Method**

Wash the okra/bhenda. Dry with a cloth & cut them into pieces of about 2 inches.

Dry roast red chillies, coriander seeds and fenugreek seeds. Grind these with grated coconut and tamarind to prepare a coarsely ground paste with very little water.

In a frying pan/kadai heat oil and add mustard seeds. When the mustard seeds crackles, add the curry leaves. Sauté them for a minute. Add the okra/bhenda and sauté them till the stickiness of okra/bhende disappears.

Add the ground coconut paste, salt and half cup water. Add salt to taste. Cover and cook on medium low heat till the water dries up and okra/benda is cooked.

## TIPS

1. One may use desi bhenda/rural okra for this curry. Those tastes better in the bhende sagle.

2. If one loves raw-ginger and onion taste, you may add ½ inch piece of finely chopped Ginger and ¼ finely chopped raw onions into the curry while the sagle is boiling.

3. Curry/Sagle with same curry paste is made with eggplant, bitter gourd/kaarate or tender cashew nuts/bibbe/kajubi

4. Okra's high levels of vitamin A, B vitamins (B1, B2, B6), and vitamin C, and traces of zinc and calcium, make it an ideal vegetable. Okra also serves as a supplement for fiber and folic acid.

# Tendle ani bibbe ukari

## Ivy gourd raw cashew stir fry

One of the delicacies served at marriage functions.

# Tendle ani bibbe ukari – Ivy gourd raw cashew stir fry

**Time**

30 Minutes

**Serves**

2-3 bowls

**Ingredients**

Ivy gourd/tendule – 200 grams
Raw cashew nuts/bibbe – 100 grams
Salt - to taste

For seasoning -
Mustard seeds - 1 teaspoon
Dry Red chillies – 1-2 to taste
Oil – 1 tablespoon

**Method**

Cut the ivy gourds lengthwise and split the tender cashew into halves.

Heat a tablespoon of oil in a large pan and season with a teaspoon of mustard seeds and dry red chillies in a thick-bottomed saucepan.

As they splutter, add the ivy gourds and cashew halves to it. Add salt to taste. Add half a cup of water. Add salt to taste. Stir to mix the ingredients together and cover with a lid. Let it all cook together till they soften. They should be cooked well but hold shape and not become mushy. Take it off the heat.

Serve hot with rice and dali toy.

**TIPS**

1. Ukari is a typical Konkani stir fry. Usually made by seasoning the vegetables and cooking with little or no water. End product will have little gravy or sometimes dry.
2. You could use dried cashew nuts as well instead of raw ones but soak them in water for about 10 minutes before you use it in the curry.
3. This is quite a healthy curry with just minimum use of oil.
4. Ivy gourd can control blood sugar levels in a natural way. This is because of the liver enzyme in the vegetable that controls the metabolism rate of sugar in the body.
5. Cashew nuts are rich in "heart-friendly" monounsaturated-fatty acids like oleic, and palmitoleic acids. These essential fatty acids help lower harmful LDL-cholesterol while increasing good HDL cholesterol in the blood.

# Nonche ambe umman

Salt pickled mango curry

# Nonche ambe umman – Salt pickled mango curry

**Time**
30 Minutes
**Serves**
2-3 bowls
**Ingredients**
Mango pickled in salt/nonche ambe – 4-5 if baby mangoes else 2
Chilli powder – 1 teaspoon to taste
Turmeric powder – 1 teaspoon
Salt - to taste, not much needed since mango is already pickled in salt
For **seasoning** -
Mustard seeds - 1 teaspoon
Fenugreek seeds – ½ teaspoon
White Lentil/Urad Dal – ½ teaspoon
Red chillies – 2 to taste
Curry leaves – 6-8
Oil – 1 tablespoon

**Method**
Remove seeds of the pickled mangoes/nonce ambe and cut the mangoes in small pieces. If the baby mangoes are quite small, you could leave them as is.

Heat a tablespoon of oil in a saucepan and season with mustard seeds, fenugreek seeds, white lentil/urad dal, red chillies and curry leaves. As they splutter, add the pickled mango pieces, chilli powder and turmeric powder.

Add about a cup of water. Add salt to taste. Stir to mix the ingredients together. Let them all simmer together for about 10 minutes.

Serve hot.

## TIPS

1. Umman is typical Konkani curry. Usually, umman is vegetables cooked with ample water to make thin gravy with curry.
2. Similar umman or curries can be made using raw mangoes, ripe mangoes, tomatoes, potatoes or mixed vegetables too.
3. It is easy to make the 'Nonche Ambe', the salted mango. Wash and wipe clean the mangoes. Boil water for about five minutes and then keep it aside to cool down. Take about 200 grams of salt, preferably salt crystal, for a kilogram of mangoes. Put them in the container and add enough boiled water to ensure that mangoes are completely immersed. Close the container and ensure it is airtight. Stir the mangoes every day, do not add any other water and ensure the mangoes are still immersed in the brine. You can add a tablespoon of oil that will float on top and ensure longer life for the 'nonche'. This should be ready in about two weeks. The mangoes will soften and its skin turn light greyish green in colour.
4. Preferably, use baby mangoes for pickling in salt.
5. The raw mangoes have a lot of nutritional value and are loaded with vitamin C and B. The presence of oxalic acid, citric acid, succinic and malice acid gives it the sour taste. It also contains pectin.

# Vaigana phodo

## Aubergine crusted with lentil curry powder

# Vaigana phodo – Aubergine crusted with lentil curry powder

**Prep Time**

30 Minutes

**Serves**

2-3 bowls

**Ingredients**

Aubergine – ½ Kg
Salt - to taste
For **seasoning** –
Chilli powder – 1 teaspoon to taste
Turmeric powder – 1 teaspoon
Mustard seeds – 1 teaspoon
Oil – 3 tablespoon
For **curry powder** -
White Lentil/Urad Dal – 2 tablespoon
Chickpea Lentil/Chana Dal – 2 tablespoon
Fenugreek seeds – ½ teaspoon
Coriander seeds – 1 tablespoon
Asafoetida – 2 pinch
Red chillies – 2 to taste
Curry leaves – 6-8
Oil – 1 teaspoon

**Method**

Roast the ingredients mentioned for the curry powder till they start to leave strong aroma and turn slight golden. Ensure it doesn't burn. Cool to room temperature and coarse grind them in a food processor. It should be grainy and not very fine powder. Keep it aside.

Cut Aubergine into 1" squares. If you have the baby ones, you can split them in four or just slit them in middle and use as is.

Heat 2 tablespoons of oil in a pan and season with mustard seeds. As they splutter, add the Aubergine pieces, chilli powder and turmeric powder. Stir around and cook them till they are a little bit soft but not mushy. Let the pieces be quite dry. Add salt to taste. Sprinkle the curry powder and keep stirring the pieces around so that they are coated all over. Add another tablespoon of oil. Let them all fry together for about 5 minutes. Take it off the heat.

Serve hot

**TIPS**
1. Phodo can be made with okra or potatoes too.
2. You could make this phodo curry powder in large quantity and use it over a few weeks.
3. This is a good way to make usually boring vegetable like aubergine taste really good. In addition to featuring a host of vitamins and minerals, aubergine or eggplant also contains important phytonutrients, many of which have antioxidant activity.

# Pappayafala sukke

Papaya stir fry

# Pappayafala sukke – Papaya stir fry

**Prep Time**

30 Minutes

**Serves**

4-5 bowl

**Ingredients**

Raw papaya – 250 grams
Small onions – 100 grams (optional)
Salt - to taste
For **seasoning** –
Mustard seeds – 1 teaspoon
Cumin seeds – 1 teaspoon
Curry leaves – 6-8
Oil – 2 tablespoon
Turmeric powder – 1 teaspoon
Asafoetida – 2 pinch
Red chilli powder – 2 to taste

**Method**

De-skin the raw papaya and grate it coarse.

Slice the small onions, thinly. If you do not have small onions, you could use normal red onions and slice them fine. Onions are optional, originally, onions were not used by GSBs.

Heat two tablespoons of oil in a saucepan and season with mustard seeds, as they splutter, add cumin seeds, turmeric powder, asafoetida and curry leaves. Sauté them a bit. Add the grated papaya and sliced onions. Add chilli powder and salt to taste. Do not add any water. If needed sprinkle a few drops. Cook covered with a lid, till papaya is soft but not mushy. Take the lid off and sauté the papaya and onions for a few minutes more. Take it off the heat.

Serve hot.

<u>TIPS</u>
1. Papayas offer not only the luscious taste and sunlit colour of the tropics, but are rich sources of antioxidant nutrients such as carotenes, vitamin C and flavonoids; the B vitamins, folate and pantothenic acid; and the minerals, potassium, copper, and magnesium; and fibre.
2. Green papayas aid digestion, converts proteins into essential amino acids, cleanses the colon, fights nausea and constipation
3. Rarely, papain, contained in papaya, in large amounts can be unsafe. It could cause allergic reaction is some people. People who might have such allergies or blood clotting disorders should avoid.
4. Green papaya contains oedema, a latex type substance, which may not be good for pregnant ladies. **Despite, so many benefits, consumption of papaya is not recommended during pregnancy.**

# Main course

# Vali ambat

Vine spinach curry

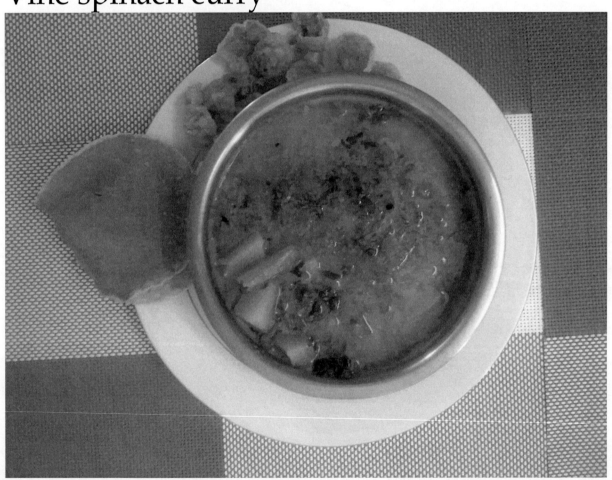

This is a popular dish in GSB households in Karnataka

# Vali ambat – Vine spinach curry

**Time**

40 Minutes

**Serves**

2-3 bowls

**Ingredients**

Vine spinach/Vali – 300 grams (approx. 3 cup leaves and 1 cup tender stems)
Tur dal/Yellow lentils – ¼ cup
Grated coconut - 1 cup
Tamarind - 1 marble size
Red chillies – 5-6 to taste
Turmeric powder – ¼ teaspoon
Onions - 2 peeled
Salt to taste
Jaggery/brown sugar - 1 tablespoon (optional)
Oil – 1 tablespoon

**Method**

Wash and pluck leaves from stems. Wash them, chop the leaves roughly and cut the tender stem 1-inch long. Finely chop the onions too.

Cook the leaves, stem and half of the diced onion along-with one small glass of water separately in a vessel. Cook the dal/lentil till soft. You could use pressure cooker to cook both but separately since dal will take more time to cook than the leaves. Add cooked dal to the cooked leaves mixture and let them boil together for a few minutes.

Lightly roast red chillies on a pan in a few drops of oil. Grind the red chillies, tamarind and coconut to a smooth paste to make the masala. Add the ground masala to the boiling dal and vali leaves mixture. Mix in salt, turmeric and optionally jaggery. Let this continue to boil for a few minutes. Add enough water to get the curry consistency.

Mix well and cook for a minute. Take it off from heat and keep aside.

Heat a teaspoon of oil in a small saucepan. Add rest of finely chopped onions. Sauté until golden brown on low flame. Add this seasoning to the cooked curry and cover the vessel with lid to contain the aroma.

**TIPS**

1. One may add cooked raw papaya or cooked potato to make the curry with phodi (vegetable pieces).
2. One may use mustard seeds and curry leaves for seasoning in place of onion. If you are a garlic lover, you may season Vali Ambat with finely chopped garlic roasted in oil instead of onion or mustard.
3. This is a healthy dish. Basella or vine spinach is very low in calories and fats. It holds an incredibly good amount of vitamins, minerals, and antioxidants, especially iron in its green leaves along with lots of fibre.

# Kadgi chakko

## Tender jackfruit stir fry

Jackfruit is one of most common vegetable used in Kerala and Karnataka. The tender ones are especially favored to make curries and stir-fry.

# Kadgi chakko – Tender jackfruit stir fry

**Time**

30 Minutes

**Serves**

3-4 bowls

**Ingredients**

Tender raw jackfruit – 250 grams

Grated coconut-1 cup

Red chillies – 3-4 to taste

Tamarind - lemon sized.

White lentil/Urad dal - 1 teaspoons

Coriander seeds – 2 teaspoons

Mustard seeds - 1 teaspoon

Curry leaves – 10-12

Salt to taste.

Oil – 2 teaspoons

Jaggery/brown sugar - 1 tablespoon (optional)

**Method**

If you have got the entire fruit and not the chopped pieces, then chop the jackfruit and peel the outer-skin of the Jackfruit. Chop-off the central ridge. Cut it into longitudinal slices of about 1 1/2 inches.

Wash the raw jack-fruit slices and pressure cook them with salt and 3/4 cups of water for 2 whistles. Do not overcook or use excess water, since we need them firm and just cooked enough.

Once cooked, drain all the water and smash them a little with hand, or you may cut them into thin pieces. Keep aside.

Fry urad dal, red chillies and coriander seeds in a few drops of oil. Grind the fried urad dal, red chillies and coriander seeds along with grated coconut, tamarind and optionally jaggery, using very little water into a coarse dry paste.

Heat teaspoon oil in a kadai or wok, add mustard seeds and curry leaves. While they are spluttering, add the ground coconut paste along with cooked jackfruit pieces. Mix well. Add ¼ cup water and close with a lid. Let it simmer for about 5 minutes till they combine well.

Add salt to taste. You will need very little since jackfruit pieces were pre-cooked with salt.

Remove from fire and serve hot with rice and dali toy.

While serving one may sprinkle a few drops of coconut oil on the chakko to give it taste and fragrance of coconut.

## TIPS

1. Pick raw jackfruit whose seeds have not started to harden.
2. Do not add too much water while cooking the jackfruit and do not over-cook also. The jackfruit should be cooked but not lose shape and there should be no gravy left, for a perfect chakko.
3. Jackfruit is a rich source of dietary fibre, antioxidants, phytonutrients and flavonoid.

# Valval

## Mixed vegetables in coconut milk

A sweetish bland curry made with coconut milk, specially made during festivals and marriages.

# Valval – Mixed vegetables in coconut milk

**Time**

45 Minutes

**Serves**

4-5 bowls

**Ingredients**

Mixed vegetables – 500 grams
(Potatoes, Mande/Arvi/Taro root,
Dudhi/Pumpkin, Ivy gourd/ Tendle, Bibbo or
tender raw cashew nuts, String Beans,
Suran/Yam, Kuwale/Ash Gourd,
Gossale/Ridge Gourd are recommended)
Green Chillies - 6 to 8 to taste
Coconut thick milk - 2 cups
Coconut thin milk - 2 cups
Water - 1 ½ cups
Salt - 1 teaspoon
Asafoetida/Hing - ½ teaspoon
Oil - 1 tablespoon
Mustard seeds - 1 teaspoon
Cumin seeds- 1 teaspoon
Curry leaves – 10-12

**Method**

Wash and peel the vegetables and cut these into cubes of 1 to 1 ½ inch.

Boil 2 cups of water in a vessel; add tough vegetables first. Cover & simmer 10 to 15 minutes till vegetables are nearly cooked.

Pour thin coconut milk into the vessel and add the rest of the tender vegetables along with the green chillies and salt. Continue to cook for another 10 to 15 minutes till all vegetables are cooked.

Once the vegetables are properly cooked, keep the flame at low and pour the thick coconut milk. Mix gently allowing it to blend into the gravy. Add salt to taste. Do not boil this curry further, otherwise the coconut milk might curdle, spoiling the gravy. Let this cook for a few minutes at very low heat and then switch off the flame.

Heat the oil in a pan; add mustard seeds and cumin seeds and allow them crackle. Then add curry leaves and hing/Asafoetida and mix well. Pour this seasoning over the curry and mix well. Serve hot with rice and dali toy.

## TIPS

1. Peel root vegetables, leave the skin on other Vegetables.

2. After adding thick milk, do not boil the curry for a long time.

3. For a variation, flavour the curry with Hing/asafoetida and 2 teaspoon coconut oil in the place of seasoning.

4. Cashew nut halves are also added to this dish along with the vegetables to make it more festive.

5. This dish, though festive, is an extremely healthy. Vegetables are full of nutrients and are an excellent source of fibre. Many are high in vitamin C, B vitamins, and vitamin A. Many are high in antioxidants.

# Chawli kadgi ghassi

Red cowpeas and jackfruit curry in coconut
sauce

A spicy curry made usually in the summers, which is the jackfruit season.

# Chawli kadgi ghassi – Red cowpeas and jackfruit curry in coconut sauce

**Time**

2 hours for soaking and 45 minutes to cook

**Serves**

3 – 4 bowls

**Ingredients**

Tender raw jackfruit – 500 grams
Chawli/red cowpeas – 100 grams
Tamarind - lemon sized
Oil – 1 teaspoon
Mustard seeds – 1 teaspoon
Curry leaves – 8-10 leaves

For curry paste or Masolu -
Grated coconut – 1 cup
Coriander seeds – 1 tablespoon (optional)
White lentil/Urad dal – 1 tablespoon (optional)
Red chillies – 4 to taste
Turmeric powder – 1 teaspoon

Salt to taste

**Method**

Chop the tender raw jackfruit into two-inch cube slices. Remove all the thorny outer skin. Use oil on your hands while chopping jackfruit to ensure that the slimy gum doesn't stick to your hands, else it would be difficult to remove later.

Soak the chawli/red cowpeas for two hours.

Soak tamarind in a cup of water

Cook the jackfruit pieces and chawli/red cowpeas separately till soft. You could use pressure cooker for this.

Grind all the ingredients mentioned in the masolu/curry paste.

In a cooking pan, heat teaspoon of oil. Put mustard seeds, as it splutters, add curry leaves. Add the cooked chawli/red cowpeas, jackfruit pieces, masolu/curry paste, tamarind soaked in water. Add salt to taste. Mix them all together. Add little water, if needed. The sauce should not be too thick but curry consistency. Let it simmer for a few minutes.

Serve hot with rice.

**TIPS**

1. Jackfruit is a rich source of dietary fibre, antioxidants, phytonutrients and flavonoid.
2. Full of protein and soluble fibre, this red cowpeas ghassi makes excellent nutritious curry for lunch.

# Kuvale kachil ambat

## Purple yam ash gourd curry in yogurt sauce

A dish popular in GSB households in Kochi side. This dish is a must to be prepared on the Diwali day - 1st day of Karthik (October/ November) month. Diwali is a very important festival for Konkanis. After having scalp massaged with coconut oil, all the family members take bath and wear new clothes.

The lady of the house prepares 5 or 7 deepams/lamp made with rice flour dough, Haldi/turmeric powder and Kum-Kumand/vermillion. The deepams/lamp are filled with oil and a wick is placed in them. Then they are kept in a row on a plate and lit up. A few small balls are also made using the same materials. The lady of the house does the aarti three times, for all family members together. Then, she will take one small ball in her hand and make two rounds - one clockwise and the other anti-clockwise, in front of each family member. She will keep the ball back on the plate and sprinkle a few drops of water on the feet of the family member. This is repeated for everyone in the family. This is supposed to remove the bad-omen. She then carries the plate out-side and throws the contents aside.

The Naivedyam/sacrament called 'Satta-Phovu' prepared with poha/aval/Beaten rice, jaggery/brown sugar, roasted Til/Sesame seed, Bengal gram, green gram and coconut. The must included dishes for Diwali feast are Khotto, Dud-Pak and 'Kuvale-Kachil Ambat.

# Kuvale kachil ambat – Purple yam ash gourd curry in yogurt sauce

**Time**

45 Minutes

**Serves**

4 - 5 bowls

**Ingredients**

Purple yam/Kachil - 250 grams
Ash Gourd/Kuvale - 250 grams
Green chillies - 5 - 7 to taste
Water - 1 cup
Salt to taste
Yogurt/Thick curd - 200ml
Grated coconut - 1 cup

For Seasoning -
Mustard Seeds - 1 teaspoon
Cumin seeds/ Jeera - ½ teaspoon
Curry Leaves – 6-8
Oil - 1 teaspoon
Red chilly - 1 to taste
Fenugreek seed/Methi - ¼ teaspoon

**Method**

Peel, wash and chop the purple yam/kachil and the ash gourd/kuvale into 1inch pieces.

Boil purple yam/kachil pieces with salt and green chillies till the kachil is soft.

Separately cook ash gourd/kuvale pieces in very little water till the pieces are soft but do not lose shape.

Grind grated coconut with 1/3 cup of water into a coarsely ground paste.

Put a deep pan on heat, add the vegetable pieces and the coconut paste. Add salt to taste. Mix well. Bring it to boil and take it off the heat.

Beat the yogurt/curd so that it is fluffy. Add to the curry. Ensure the curry is off the heat. The curry should not boil once the curd is added because curd could split, spoiling the curry.

In a small pan, heat teaspoon of oil. Add mustard seeds. As it splutters, add fenugreek seeds, cumin seeds, red chilly and curry leaves. Sauté for a minute.

Garnish the kuvale-kachil ambat with this seasoning and serve hot with rice.

**TIPS**

1. If Kachil (Purple yam) is not available, you may use Taro root/Colocasia root/Arbi or usual Yam. Both taste very similar to Kachil (Purple yam).

2. These root vegetables are full of nutrients and are an excellent source of fibre. Many are high in vitamin C, B vitamins, and vitamin A. Many are high in antioxidants.

# Soi bhajili ghassi

## Mix vegetable curry in fried coconut sauce

One of the delicacies served at marriage functions or when guests are visiting.

# Soi bhajili ghassi – Mix vegetable curry in fried coconut sauce

**Prep Time**

60 Minutes

**Serves**

4-5 Persons

**Ingredients**

Yam/Suran – 200 grams
Potatoes – 200 grams
Cauliflower – 200 grams
Black chickpea/Kala Chono – ½ cup
Garcinia/Gambooge/kudampuli/ Dharbein sol – 2 pieces
Salt - to taste
For curry paste or **Masolu** -
Grated coconut – 1 cup
Coriander seeds – 1 tablespoon
White lentil/Urad dal – 1 tablespoon
Red chillies – 2 to taste

**Method**

Roast the grated coconut on a low flame till it starts to leave strong aroma and turn golden. Ensure it doesn't burn or turn dark brown. Keep stirring. All the moisture of coconut should evaporate completely for long shelf life of this curry paste. Add other ingredients mentioned for the curry paste or Masolu and roast for a few minutes more on low flame. Cool to room temperature and grind them in a food processor to an extremely fine paste. Do not add any water at all. You'd notice that coconut would start leaving oil as you grind it. Keep it aside.

Clean, skin and cut all the vegetables into 1" square. Cook them till they are a little bit soft but not mushy. Cook the black chickpea/kala chono also till soft. You could use a pressure cooker for this.

In a deep pan boil two tablespoons of the curry paste or Masolu along with the Garcinia pieces and a cup of water. Add the black chickpea/kala chono and the cooked vegetables. Add water if need be to get a thick curry consistency. Add salt to taste. Let them all simmer together for about 5 minutes. Take it off the heat. Serve hot.

**TIPS**

1. Ghassi is any curry made with ground coconut paste. This one is a special one made with coconut paste that has been roasted or bhajile as in Konkani.
2. This curry paste or Masolu has a long shelf life. You can stock it up in a refrigerator for a few months. This is also called red curry or tambadi ghassi for the dark red color of the curry due to golden brown roasted coconut paste with red chillies.
3. This curry or ghassi can be made with any set of vegetables of one's liking but goes very well with beans, lentils and root vegetables. Breadfruit also one of the popular ingredients.
4. You can use tamarind as souring agent if you do not have Dharbein sol.
5. You might think of this to be high calorie due to frying of coconut but actually it's fried in its own oil, thus, this is quite healthy. Mix of vegetables and lentils gives it a healthy edge by providing good source of carbohydrates, fibre and proteins.

# Dhavi ghassi

Mix vegetable curry in coconut sauce

# Dhavi ghassi – Mix vegetable curry in coconut sauce

**Prep Time**

45 Minutes

**Serves**

4-5 Persons

**Ingredients**

Yam/Suran – 200 grams
Potatoes – 200 grams
Cauliflower – 200 grams
Yellow Lentils/Tur dal – ½ cup
Garcinia/Gambooge/kudampuli/
Dharbein sol – 2 pieces
Salt - to taste
For curry paste or **Masolu** -
Grated coconut – 1 cup
Coriander seeds – 1 tablespoon
White lentil/Urad dal – 1 tablespoon
Red chillies – 2 to taste
Turmeric powder – 1 teaspoon

**Method**

Grind all the ingredients for curry paste or Masolu in a food processor to a fine paste. Keep it aside.

Clean, skin and cut all the vegetables into 1" square. Cook them till they are a little bit soft but not mushy. Cook the yellow lentil/Tur dal also till soft. You could use a pressure cooker for this.

Heat a tablespoon of oil in a deep pan and season with a teaspoon of mustard seeds, cumin seeds and curry leaves. As they splutter, add the cooked dal, pumpkin and coconut paste to it. Add water to get a thick curry consistency. Add salt to taste. Stir to mix the ingredients together. Let it all simmer together for about 10 minutes. Take it off the heat. Serve hot.

<u>TIPS</u>
1. Ghassi is curry made with ground coconut paste. Its called white or dhavi in Konkani since it is made with white ground fresh coconut paste or Masolu.
2. You can use tamarind as souring agent if you do not have Dharbein sol.
3. Mix of vegetables and lentils gives it a healthy edge by providing good source of carbohydrates, fibre and proteins.

# Teeksani umman

## Mix vegetable curry in spicy hot sauce

One of the quick, simple and spicy curries, made often in GSB households.

# Teeksani umman – Mix vegetable curry in spicy hot sauce

**Prep Time**
30 Minutes
**Serves**
4-5 bowls
**Ingredients**
Purple Yam/Kachil – 200 grams
Potatoes – 100 grams
Bitter gourd – 50 grams
Yardlong beans – 50 grams
jackfruit seeds – 50 grams
Garcinia/Gambooge/
kudampuli/Dharbein sol – 2 pieces
Salt - to taste
For **curry paste** -
Red chillies – 5 to taste
Turmeric powder – 1 teaspoon
Asafoetida – 2 pinch
For **seasoning** –
Turmeric powder – 1 teaspoon
Mustard seeds – 1 teaspoon
Curry leaves – 8-10 leaves
Oil – 1 tablespoon

**Method**
Grind all the ingredients for curry paste with a little water in a food processor to a fine paste. Keep it aside.

Clean, de-skin and cut all the vegetables into 1" square.

In a deep pan, boil a tablespoon of the curry paste along with the Garcinia pieces and a cup of water. Add the vegetables. Add little water to get a thick curry consistency. Cook them till they are a little bit soft but not mushy. You could use a pressure cooker for this. Take it off the heat.

In a pan, heat oil. Put mustard seeds, as it splutters, add curry leaves and turmeric powder. Sauté for a minute and add the cooked vegetables with the curry. Add salt to taste. Let it simmer for a few minutes, and then take it off the flame.

Serve hot.

**TIPS**
1. Umman is a simple curry made of vegetable cooked with little water. This is a special curry or umman made extra spicy by adding spicy chilly paste.
2. Teeksani Umman can be made with other vegetables also like potatoes, root vegetables, tomato, and mango pickled in salt or simple mixed vegetables.
3. If you like to make the curry sour along with spicy hot, you could use tamarind water or a few sour tomatoes instead of Garcina/Dharbein sol.
4. This is a healthy recipe and good way to include vegetables in your daily diet. Vegetables are important sources of many nutrients, including potassium, dietary fibre, folate (folic acid), vitamin A, and vitamin C.

# Alchikari

Lentil and pumpkin curry

# Alchikari – Lentil and pumpkin curry

**Prep Time**

45 Minutes

**Serves**

4-5 bowls

**Ingredients**

Red pumpkin – 250 grams
Green lentil/Moong dal – 100 grams
Salt - to taste
For **seasoning** –
Mustard seeds – 1 teaspoon
Cumin seeds – 1 teaspoon
Curry leaves – 6-8
Oil – 1 tablespoon
For **coconut paste** –
Grated coconut – 1 cup
Turmeric powder – 1 teaspoon
Asafoetida – 2 pinch
Red chillies – 2 to taste

**Method**

Grind all the ingredients for the coconut paste in a food processor, into a fine paste.

De-skin the pumpkin and cut in 1" cubes. Cook green lentil/Moong dal and pumpkin separately till soft. You could use a pressure cooker for this.

Heat a tablespoon of oil in a saucepan and season with mustard seeds, as they splutter, add cumin seeds and curry leaves. Sauté them a bit. Add the cooked pumpkin, lentil and the coconut paste. Add little water to get a thick curry consistency. Add salt to taste. Let them all simmer together for about 10 minutes. Take it off the heat.

Serve hot.

**TIPS**

1. Alchikari can be made with yellow lentils/toor dal and another root vegetable like yam, purple yam or potatoes. Alchikari is usually made with one type of lentil and one type of root vegetable with ground coconut paste.
2. Lentils and pumpkin are both quite healthy ingredients. Pumpkin is a source of dietary fibre and minerals like copper, calcium, potassium and phosphorus. Lentils are the best source of proteins from plants. They are a must in the daily diet for the vegetarians.

# Chutneys

# Alle tambali

## Ginger Chutney

No festival meal is complete without this digestive aid.

# Alle tambali – Ginger chutney

**Prep Time**

15 Minutes

**Serves**

16 tablespoons

**Ingredients**

Coarse grated ginger - 6" piece
Fine grated coconut – 1 cup
Crushed green chillies – 1-2 to taste
Salt - to taste
For **seasoning** -
Mustard seeds - 1 teaspoon
Curry leaves – 6-8
Oil – 1 tablespoon

**Method**

Heat a tablespoon of oil and season with a teaspoon of mustard seeds and curry leaves. Once they start to splutter, add the grated ginger and sauté it for a few minutes. Added grated coconut and crushed green chillies. Add salt to taste.

You may simply grind fresh coconut, ginger and chillies all together in a food processor to a coarse paste instead of grating or crushing them.

Add a little water to get it to a chutney consistency. Stir to mix the ingredients for a few more minutes and take it off the heat. Serve at room temperature.

<u>TIPS</u>

1.  This is a very healthy recipe with ginger as main ingredient that helps in digestion and has many other health benefits too.
2.  You may use tamarind water or curd instead of coconut paste for another type of Alle with crisp hot and sour taste.
3.  You may even add a little bit of grated jiggery/brown sugar when making Alle with tamarind water. A bit of sweet along with hot and sour creates unique tasting chutney.

# Nonche ambe tambali

## Salted Mango Chutney

It is easy to make the 'Nonche Ambe', the salted mango. Wash and wipe clean the mangoes. Boil water for about five minutes and then keep it aside to cool down. Take about 200 grams of salt, preferably salt crystal, for a kilogram of mangoes. Put them in the container and add enough water to ensure that mangoes are completely immersed. Close the container and ensure it is airtight. Stir the mangoes every day, do not add any other water and ensure the mangoes are still immersed in the brine. You can add tablespoon oil that will float on top and ensure longer life for the 'nonche'. This should be ready in about two weeks. The mangoes will soften and its skin turn light greyish green in color.

# Nonche ambe tambali – Salted mango chutney

**Prep Time**

15 Minutes

**Serves**

16 tablespoons

**Ingredients**

Mango pickled in salt – 2-3 if baby mangoes else 1

Fine grated coconut – 1 cup

Crushed green chillies – 1-2 to taste

Salt - to taste, not much needed since mango is already pickled in salt

For **seasoning** -

Mustard seeds - 1 teaspoon

Curry leaves – 6-8

Oil – 1 tablespoon

**Method**

Remove skin and seed of the pickled mangoes and smash them into pulp using a spoon or fork.

Add the grated coconut and crushed green chillies.

Grind them to paste in a food processor. Add salt to taste. Add a little water to get it to a chutney consistency.

Heat a tablespoon of oil in a small pan and season with a teaspoon of mustard seeds and curry leaves. Let them splutter.

Add to the pickled mango paste. Stir to mix the ingredients together. Serve at room temperature with dosa, idli, and chapattis or in sandwiches.

**TIPS**

1. Ensure that the mangoes pickled in salt are really soft and pulpy. Hard pickled mangoes are not ready yet. Wait for a few more days for them to become soft, before you use them.
2. You could use raw mangoes too but they would have to be cooked before adding to the coconut paste. Just boil or pressure cook them till they are soft.
3. Similar chutneys can be made using gooseberries or lemons pickled in salt.
4. This is a healthy way to incorporate antioxidants and vitamins in the diet. Mangoes, gooseberries and lemons are good source of many antioxidants and vitamins especially vitamin C.

# Kothambari palya gojju

## Coriander leaves chutney

This dish is usually part of all festival feast menus as a side dish in Konkani homes.

# Kottambari palya gojju – Coriander leaves chutney

**Prep Time**

15 minutes

**Serves**

2 -3 bowls

**Ingredients**

Coriander Leaves – 1 bunch or 250 grams
Jaggery/brown sugar– 4-5 tablespoons
Red chillies - 3 - 4 to taste
Tamarind – 1 marble sized
Salt to taste
For **Seasoning**-
Oil – 1 Teaspoon
Mustard seeds - 1/2 Teaspoon
Curry leaves – 8-10 leaves

**Method**

Wash the coriander leaves and chop roughly including the stem;

Dry roast the red chillies.

Grind the leaves with tamarind, jiggery/brown sugar, roasted chillies and salt into a medium thick paste using little water.

Heat teaspoon oil in a pan. Add mustard seeds. Once they start to splutter, add curry leaves.

Add this seasoning to the ground leaves.

Serve it with the main course or as a dip with starters.

You may refrigerate it for further use.

**TIPS**

1. You may add 2 – 3 teaspoons of grated coconut while grinding in order to make a variation.
2. You may adjust the Jaggery/brown sugar and chillies according to your taste.

# Tomato gojju

## Tomato curry

A quick and spicy dish, commonly prepared in a GSB home.

# Tomato gojju – Tomato curry

**Prep Time**

20 Minutes

**Serves**

3 to 4 bowls

**Ingredients**

Fully Ripe Tomatoes - 3 big sized.
Potatoes - 2 medium sized.
Green chillies - 2 - 3 to taste
Hing/Asafoetida – ½ teaspoon.
Coriander Leaves – 5-6
For seasoning-
Mustard - 1 teaspoon.
Curry Leaves - 4 to 5.
Asafoetida/Hing - one pinch.
Oil – 1 teaspoon

**Method**

Boil or pressure-cook the tomatoes and potatoes till it is soft. Remove the skin of potatoes. Mash cooked tomatoes and potatoes to a coarse paste. Crush the green chilles and add it along with salt and Hing powder.

To give it a thick curry consistency, add water as needed. Normally this Gojju is not watery but thick curry. Keep this aside.

In small pan heat teaspoon oil, add mustard seeds and curry leaves. As it splutters, add the asafoetida/hing in it.

Add this seasoning into the Gojju and mix well.

Serve hot garnished with chopped coriander leaves.

TIPS

1. Without seasoning also, this Gojjju tastes good, by giving a garnish of pinch of Hing and 1 ½ tablespoons of coconut oil.
2. One may add 2 tablespoons of thick curd to enhance the sourness of the Gojju.
3. Tomatoes are one of the healthiest foods, making them a must in daily diet. Tomatoes are an excellent source vitamin C, biotin, molybdenum, and vitamin K. They are also a very good source of copper, potassium, manganese, dietary fiber, vitamin A (in the form of beta-carotene), vitamin B6, folate, niacin, vitamin E, and phosphorus.

# Ambo chirdilo

## Ripe mango chutney

# Ambo chirdilo – Ripe mango chutney

**Time**

15 Minutes

**Serves**

10 tablespoons

**Ingredients**

Ripe Mango - 1
Sugar – 1 tablespoon
Crushed green chillies – 1-2 to taste
Salt - to taste

**Method**

Peel the skin and remove seed of the ripe mango. Smash the fruit to pulpy paste using a spoon or a fork.
Add the crushed green chillies with sugar. Add salt to taste.

Serve at room temperature. Goes very well with rice, poori, chapattis or rice. You could use them in sandwiches to give them interesting sweet and spicy twist.

<u>TIPS</u>
1. Ensure that the mango is really ripe, soft and pulpy.
2. You could use packaged mango pulp as well if fresh ripe fruit is not available.
3. Due to its juicy sweet taste, mango is called king of fruits. Though a variety of mango called Alphonso is the king of mangoes but this recipe comes out really well with local south Indian mango variety called Moovandan, Malgova or naadan.
4. Mangoes are full of nutrients especially vitamin C, folate and beta-carotene. In case of mangoes, this extremely sweet fruit is very good for your health too!

# Nonche avale sassam

## Salted gooseberry chutney

It is easy to make the 'Nonche Aavale', the salted gooseberry. Wash and wipe clean the gooseberries. Boil water for about five minutes and then keep it aside to cool down. Take about 200 grams of salt, preferably salt crystal, for a kilogram of gooseberries. Put them in the container and add enough water to ensure that gooseberries are completely immersed. Close the container and ensure it is airtight. Stir the mangoes every day, do not add any other water and ensure the gooseberries are still immersed in the brine. You can add tablespoon oil that will float on top and ensure longer life for the 'nonche'. This should be ready in about two weeks. The gooseberries will soften and its skin turn light greyish yellow in color.

# Nonche avale sassam – Salted gooseberry chutney

**Time**

15 Minutes

**Serves**

16 tablespoons

**Ingredients**

Gooseberries pickled in salt – 4
Fine grated coconut – ½cup
Curd or yogurt – ½ cup
Crushed green chillies – 1-2 to taste
Salt - to taste, not much needed since gooseberry is already pickled in salt
For **seasoning** -
Mustard seeds - 1 teaspoon
Curry leaves – 6-8
Oil – 1 tablespoon

**Method**

Remove seeds of the pickled gooseberries and smash them into pulp using a spoon or fork.

Add the grated coconut and crushed green chillies. Grind them to paste in a food processor.

Add curd or yogurt to get it to a chutney consistency. Add salt to taste.

Heat a tablespoon of oil in a small pan and season with a teaspoon of mustard seeds and curry leaves. Add to the pickled gooseberries paste. Stir to mix the ingredients together.

Serve at room temperature.

**TIPS**

1. Ensure that the salted gooseberries are soft.
2. You could use raw gooseberries too; cook them before you use them in the recipe. Just boil or pressure-cook them till they are soft and squishy.
3. Add curd or yogurt quantity based on its consistency. End product should not flow but chutney consistency.
4. You can make this recipe with raw gooseberries or mangoes too. Do cook them well till they very soft before you use them in this recipe.
5. You could make this with ripe fruits like pineapple or banana too.
6. It would not be wrong to call Indian gooseberries, super food. They are packed with antioxidants and vitamins especially vitamin C. In the ancient texts, it is rightly called as "sarvadosha hara - a remover of all diseases". This is highly recommended as essential part of daily meals.

# Pickles

# Surna adgai

Yam pickle

Yam pickle made in this Konkani style is also known as surna pachetti or nonche. It is served as accompaniment with rice, khotto, moode, idli or dosa.

# Surna adgai – Yam pickle

**Time**

45 Minutes

**Serves**

32 tablespoons

**Ingredients**

Suran/Yam - 1 cup
Red Chillies - 12 - 15
Tamarind - Lemon sized.
Methi/Fenugreek seeds – ¼ teaspoon
Mustard seeds - 1 teaspoon
Hing/Asafoetida – ½ teaspoon
Salt to taste
Coriander seeds - 1 teaspoon (optional)
Oil - for frying
Curry leaves – 8 – 10 leaves

**Method**

Peel, wash and chop the suran/yam to very small pieces. Apply salt to the chopped yam; keep aside for 30 minutes.

Squeeze out the excess water from the yam and deep fry till crisp. Keep this aside.

Roast red chillies, methi/fenugreek seeds, half of the mustard seeds and coriander seeds in a teaspoon of oil.

Grind roasted red chillies, tamarind, hing/asafoetida, roasted methi/fenugreek seeds, roasted mustard and coriander seeds into a smooth paste. To bring this into right consistency you may add ½ cup of water while grinding.

Boil this paste for 10 minutes. Take off the flame and add the fried yam pieces to this paste.

Heat teaspoon oil in a pan. Add ½ teaspoon of mustard seeds. As they start to splutter, add curry leaves.

Season the yam pickle with this seasoned oil.

You may add more salt, according to taste.

## TIPS

1. The red chillies may be increased or decreased as per one's taste.

2. A bit of jaggery/brown sugar may be added to reduce the pungency of the red chillies.

3. Add mustard and methi seeds carefully, too much of this would make the adgai bitter.

4. While adding salt, remember that the suran/yam pieces were already marinated in salt.

5. Although yam is considered to be a starchy vegetable, yams are made up of complex carbohydrates and dietary fiber allowing for slow uptake to keep blood sugar levels even, giving it the nod as a low glycemic index food. Yam also provides good amounts of fiber, potassium, manganese, and metabolic B vitamins.

# Ambe adgai

## Instant mango pickle

# Ambe adgai – Instant mango pickle

## Time

15 Minutes

## Serves

16 tablespoons

## Ingredients

Raw mango – 1 large one or 200 grams
Salt – 2 tablespoons to taste
Red chilli powder – 2 tablespoons to taste
Turmeric powder – 1 teaspoon
Asafoetida – 2 pinch
Oil – 1 teaspoon

## Method

Clean, deseed and finely chop the mango along with its skin.

Add rest of the ingredients to the finely chopped mango and mix well.

## TIPS

1. The red chillies may be increased or decreased as per one's taste.

2. A bit of Jaggery/brown sugar may be added to reduce the pungency of the red chillies.

3. The raw mango is highly appreciated for its nutritional value they are excellent source of Vitamin C. An unripe mango supposedly yields as much Vitamin C as 35 apples, 18 bananas, nine lemons and three oranges. Due to the presence of vitamin C, they are highly beneficial in strengthening immune system. Raw mango is rich in vitamin A and C, calcium, iron and magnesium.

# Nimbuye adgai

## Instant lemon pickle

# Nimbuye adgai – Instant lemon pickle

**Time**

15 Minutes

**Serves**

16 tablespoons

**Ingredients**

Lemon – 4 large ones or 100 grams
Salt - to taste
Ginger – 1"
Green chilli – 2 to taste
Red chilli powder – 1 tablespoon to taste
Turmeric powder – 1 teaspoon
Asafoetida – 2 pinch
Mustard seeds – 1 teaspoon
Oil – 2 teaspoon

**Method**

Wash and clean the lemons. Do not chop them yet. Chop chilli and ginger coarsely.

In a frying pan, heat oil. Sauté the lemons till golden. Remove from the pan and keep them aside to cool down.

In the pan, put the mustard seeds in the rest of the oil. Add turmeric powder and Asafoetida to this oil, once the mustard seeds start to spurt. Also add the chopped ginger and chilli. Sauté for a few minutes and take it off the flame.

Once the lemons have cooled, chop them along with its skin to six to eight parts.

Add the chopped lemons to the rest of ingredients in the seasoned oil and mix well.

## TIPS

1. Be careful while sautéing the lemons, they might crack spluttering the oil.
2. Lemons are full of nutrients like vitamin C, vitamin B6, vitamin A, vitamin E, folate, niacin thiamin, riboflavin, pantothenic acid, copper, calcium, iron, magnesium, potassium, zinc, phosphorus and protein. Lemon is a fruit that contains flavonoids, which are composites that contain antioxidants. Lemon has proved to be nature's boon to everyone who uses it. Lemon pickle is a must in daily diet for all its amazing health benefits.

# Nonche ambe adgai

## Salted mango pickle

# Nonche ambe adgai – Salted mango pickle

**Time**

15 Minutes

**Serves**

16 tablespoons

**Ingredients**

Salted mango – 1 large one or 200 grams
Red chilli powder – 2 tablespoons to taste
Turmeric powder – 1 teaspoon
Asafoetida – 2 pinch
Oil – 1 teaspoon

**Method**

Wash and clean the salted mango. Coarsely chop the mango along with its skin. You may choose to keep the mango seed intact or discard it.

Add rest of the ingredients to the mango pieces and mix well.

**TIPS**

1. It is easy to make the 'Nonche Ambe', the salted mango. Wash and wipe clean the mangoes. Boil water for about five minutes and then keep it aside to cool down. Take about 200 grams of salt, preferably salt crystal, for a kilogram of mangoes. Put them in the container and add enough water to ensure that mangoes are completely immersed. Close the container and ensure it is airtight. Stir the mangoes every day, do not add any other water and ensure the mangoes are still immersed in the brine. You can add tablespoon oil that will float on top and ensure longer life for the 'nonche'. This should be ready in about two weeks. The mangoes will soften and its skin turn light greyish green in colour.
2. The 'nonche' made with 'ambuli', the tender tiny raw mangoes are even tastier and most popular in GSB homes.
3. No salt is needed in this recipe since the mangoes are already salted.
4. The raw mango is highly appreciated for its nutritional value they are excellent source of Vitamin C. An unripe mango supposedly yields as much Vitamin C as 35 apples, 18 bananas, nine lemons and three oranges. Due to the presence of vitamin C, they are highly beneficial in strengthening immune system. Raw mango is rich in vitamin A and C, calcium, iron and magnesium.

# Nonche aavale adgai

Salted gooseberry pickle

# Nonche aavale adgai – Salted gooseberry pickle

**Time**

15 Minutes

**Serves**

16 tablespoons

**Ingredients**

Salted gooseberries – 8-10 or 200 grams

Red chilli powder – 2 tablespoons to taste

Turmeric powder – 1 teaspoon

Asafoetida – 2 pinch

Oil – 1 teaspoon

**Method**

Wash and clean the salted gooseberries. Remove the seeds and split apart the segments. Chop the segments into two pieces.

Add rest of the ingredients to the finely chopped mango and mix well.

TIPS

1. Gooseberries are extremely healthy. It is supposed to be the richest source of the antioxidant vitamin C. Every 100 grams of fresh gooseberry provides nearly 700 mg of this vitamin that is 20 times higher than what is found in an orange. Also, the presence of compounds like polyphenols, minerals like Iron and zinc and vitamins like Carotenes and Vitamin B complex in amla prevents various diseases.
2. No salt is needed in this recipe since the gooseberries are already salted.
3. It is easy to make the 'Nonche Aavale', the salted gooseberries. Wash and wipe clean the gooseberries. Boil water for about five minutes and then keep it aside to cool down. Take about 200 grams of salt, preferably salt crystal, for a kilogram of gooseberries. Put them in the container and add enough water to ensure that mangoes are completely immersed. Close the container and ensure it is airtight. Stir the gooseberries every day, do not add any other water and ensure the gooseberries are still immersed in the brine. You can add tablespoon oil that will float on top and ensure longer life for the 'nonche'. This should be ready in about two weeks. The gooseberries will soften and its skin turn light greyish yellow in colour.

# Tambale puddi

## Spicy chutney powder

Tambale puddi is a Konkani side dish used as an alternative to a pickle. It is a must in any feast given by GSB families. The spicy powder goes very well with rice and curries.

# Tambale puddi – Spicy chutney powder

**Prep Time**

60 minutes

**Serves**

600-700 gram powder

**Ingredients**

Grated coconut – 3 cup
Chana dal/Gram lentils - 300 grams
Urad dal/White lentils - 250 grams
Coriander seeds - 1 tablespoon (optional)
Jeera/cumin seeds - 1 teaspoon (optional)
Dry red chillies – 12-14 to taste
Tamarind – 1 small marble size
Curry leaves – 20-25
Salt to taste

**Method**

Dry roast the grated coconut, dry red chillies and curry leaves together on low heat till golden brown. Remove from the pan and keep this aside. In the same pan, slightly fry the tamarind with salt.

Dry roast the dals/lentils, separately, till golden brown. Dry roast coriander seeds and jeera/cumin seeds till you get a nice fragrance. Keep them aside also, to cool down.

When the dals/lentils, coriander and jeera/cumin seeds come to room temperature, grind them together to a semi-coarse powder. Keep aside.

Grind the fried coconut mixture in a food processor till it becomes a fine powder and the oil separates. Add to this the slightly fried tamarind and salt and grind again till they mix well. To this mixture, add the dal mixture powder, little by little and mix them together with hand. The end product should be a fragrant fine brown powder.

Thambale Puddi is ready to be served.

**TIPS**

1. If kept in a dry air-tight container, Tambale Puddi can be used for a month or so.

2. Thambale Puddi is great to be eaten with Pej (Rice Porridge).

3. The coconut used should be fully ripe one with least or no water in it. One can use dry coconut/copra also for this recipe, even though it is not that much preferred.

4. Use the dry type of tamarind instead of soft paste or liquid type.

4. Each family usually has their own recipe for Tambale puddi. Some use more urad dal and less chana dal; others vice versa. GSBs in Karnataka use more of coriander seeds. You can try to make your own combination for tastiest spicy chutney powder.

# Karambala torro

## Starfruit pickle

# Karambala torro – Starfruit pickle

## Time

30 minutes to sauté, overnight in brine, 4 hours for drying and a week to pickle

## Serves

500grams pickle

## Ingredients

Raw starfruit – 500 grams

Red chillies – 100 grams to taste

Salt – 1 tablespoon to taste

Crystal salt – 2 tablespoons to taste

Asafoetida/Hing – 1 teaspoon

Oil – 5 tablespoons

## Method

Wash and pat dry the starfruits. Remove the edges and ends. Slit them vertically to about half-length of the fruit. If fruit is of bigger size, then split them into long wedges of about 2-inch length.

Sprinkle the crystal salt on them and set it aside for a few hours preferably overnight. Stir it around often so that all fruit pieces get coated well. Keep it aside overnight. Next day drain all the liquid. Tie the brined fruit pieces in a cheesecloth. Hang it up to dry. Instead of hanging to dry, you could dry it out in sun or place the bundle under a heavy stone mortar & pestle so that, as much as possible, water content of the fruit pieces is removed. This could take about 4-6 hours.

Heat a thick pan with two tablespoons of oil in it and put the brined and dried starfruit pieces in it. Keep the flame to minimum. Roast the fruit till all water evaporates and it becomes slightly crisp. Keep it aside to cool. Do not cover other wise precipitated steam will moisturize the fruits spoiling the chance of pickle to last longer.

In same pan dry roast, the chillies. Grind them to fine powder in a food processor. Add salt and asafoetida to the chilli powder.

Once the brined, dried and roasted starfruits are at room temperature, add the chilli powder, salt and Asafoetida mixture to it. Stir them around so that all pieces are completely coated with the chilli mixture.

Take 3 tablespoons oil in a small pan and heat it to the smoking point. Drizzle this over the pickled starfruit. Stir around some more so that all chilli powder get stuck to the fruits. Keep this aside for a week to pickle in an airtight container that is moisture free.

## TIPS

1. Small and green, really tender & raw starfruit is best for making this torro pickle.
2. If you do not have crystal salt, you can use normal salt to brine. You could use normal chilli powder instead of chillies as well. Be careful about the amount of salt used in pickling since the starfruit is already brined in salt.
3. Ensure that the brined starfruit is dried very well. Lesser the moisture in starfruit while pickling, longer time the pickle will stay fresh.
4. Star fruit contains good quantities of Vitamin-C and is rich in antioxidant phyto-nutrient polyphenolic flavonoids. It is a good source of B-complex vitamins such as folates, riboflavin, and pyridoxine

# Sweets

# Haldi panna pathali

Sweet rice dumpling in turmeric leaf

This dessert is prepared in GSB homes for Gowri pooja, Ganesh chaturthi and Nagar pachami festivals.

# Haldi panna pathali – Sweet rice dumpling in turmeric leaf

**Time**

60 Minutes and 4 hours for soaking

**Serves**

15 - 20 dumplings

**Ingredients**

Turmeric leaves - 20

Raw rice - 1 cup

Salt – ¼ teaspoon

Elaichi/cardamom powder – ½ teaspoon

Jaggery/brown sugar – ¾ cup

Grated coconut - 1 ½ cup

**Method**

Wash and soak the raw rice in 3 cups of water for 4 hours. Grind the soaked raw rice to a slightly thick batter that is not runny. Keep aside.

For the filling - In another pan, heat ¼ cup of water and add the jiggery. Cook till you get a think syrup (Godda Pankh). Then add the grated coconut and mix well, and cook till it becomes completely dry. Now sprinkle the elaichi/cardamom powder into the filling and mix well.

Wash the turmeric leaves and remove the stalks.

Take tablespoon of rice batter and spread it along the center of the leaf lengthwise. Now take ½ tablespoon of the filling and place it along the center of the rice batter. Fold the Turmeric leaf length-wise by following its spine. Follow this procedure for all the haldi leaves and keep aside.

Heat 3 cups of water in a steamer/ pedavan and bring it to boil. Place all the prepared Patholis gently in the steamer or pedavan; close the lid and cook it on medium flame for 15 minutes.

Turn off the flame and leave it to cool for 5 to 8 minutes.

Serve hot with ghee or clarified butter.

## TIPS

1. The amount of batter and filling ratio can be changed according to your taste. If you like it more sweet, you may increase the filling.

2. To make the patholis softer, while grinding the raw rice add ¼ to ½ cup of grated coconut and 2 tablespoon jaggery with the raw rice.

3. If the haldi leaves are not available, you may make the rice batter thicker, more like a dough and make dumplings with hands, fill the sweet mixture inside the dumpling and steam them. In Konkani this is called Poornodo. However, you will not get the fragrance of the haldi. You may use a banana leaf piece or any other leaves as well.

# Madagane

## Broken wheat pudding

Madagane or Gova-Kena Godshe, is a Konkani Kheer, a traditional sweet pudding, made on the occasion of Sanvsaar-Padvo/ Yugadi.

# Madagane – Broken wheat pudding

**Time**
1 hour and 5 hours for soaking
**Serves**
6 - 8 bowls
**Ingredients**
Dalia/broken wheat (Gova-Kena) – 1 ½ cup Optionally use Chana dal
Molten Jaggery /brown sugar– 1 cup (or jaggery broken into small pieces)
Elaichi/cardamom powder – ½ teaspoon
Rice flour – 2 tablespoons optional (to thicken)
Grated coconut – 2 cups
Water as per consistency
Cashew nuts – 10-12

**Method**
Preparing **coconut milk** – Grind the grated coconut with water and extract the first/thick coconut milk by squeezing out the milk from the paste. Keep this thick milk aside. Add one cup water to the same grated coconut left after extracting thick milk, grind again and extract the thin milk by squeezing out the milk from the paste. Repeat this procedure third time and extract the thin milk once again.

If using chana dal, then soak the chana dal in water for 5 hours. Drain the water in which it was soaked.

Add enough water to completely immerse the broken wheat/soaked chana dal and cashew nuts. Pressure cook till 2 whistles or cook it in a pan till soft and mushy.

To this mixture add jaggery. Once jaggery melts completely and mixes with the mixture, add the thin milk. Bring to boil and adjust the consistency while keeping on stirring it gently. Now add the thick coconut milk and cook on slow flame. If the consistency is too thin, add a paste made of rice flour with water into the kheer, while you continue to stir. Constant stirring is required to avoid lumps and kheer sticking to the bottom.

Bring to a complete boil once and turn off the flame. Garnish with elaichi/cardamom powder.

Madgane or Gova-Kone Godshe/ Kheer is ready to be served.

<u>TIPS</u>
1. Madagane can be served hot or chilled. If chilled, this tastes like coconut pudding.
2. Instead of raw cashew nuts, one may use fried cashew nuts in ghee; this will add nice aroma to the Madagane.
3. Broken wheat is a good source of fiber, magnesium, iron, and phosphorus. It provides an improved glycemic index than refined flour or white rice, but as a sweet, it should be eaten in moderation.

# Cheppe kheeri

## Unsweetened rice pudding

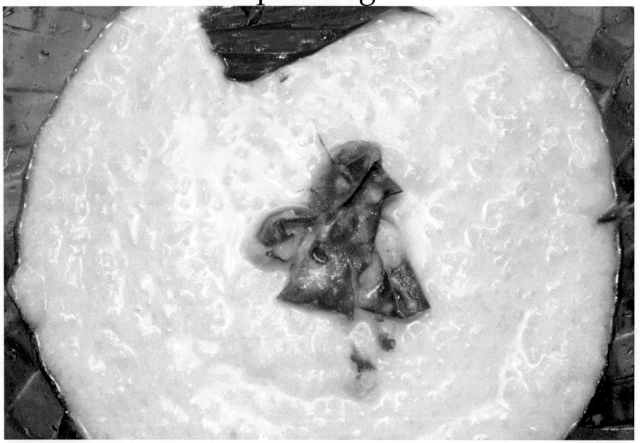

An un-sweetened Rice Pudding (Cheppe Kheeri) specially made on Ganesh Chathurthi and Nagar-Panchami in Konkani GSB Homes.

Cheppe Kheeri can also be sweetened by adding sugar or jaggery, according to taste, if one doesn't like to have this cheppe i.e. Unsweetened.

# Cheppe kheeri – Unsweetened rice pudding

**Time**
45 minutes
**Serves**
2-3 bowl
**Ingredients**
Sohna-Masuri Rice or Basmati or any fragrant rice according to one's taste – ½ cup.
Haldi/ Turmeric leaves – 2 leaves.
Water to cook the rice
Grated coconut – 2 cups

**Method**
Preparing **coconut milk** – Grind the grated coconut with half a cup water and extract the first/ thick coconut milk by squeezing out the milk from the paste. Keep this thick milk aside. Add one cup water to the same grated coconut left after extracting think milk, grind again and extract the thin milk by squeezing out the milk from the paste. Repeat this procedure third time and extract the thin milk once again.

Wash rice and drain water. Add required water for cooking. Once the rice is half cooked, add the thin coconut milk into it and boil further until you get a soft cooked rice. Add the Haldi/ Turmeric leaves into the rice and let the Haldi flavor mix in to the Kheeri.

Add the thick coconut milk and bring the contents to boil over low flame, bringing it to the right consistency.

Remove from heat and the Cheppe-Kheeri is ready to serve.

TIPS
1. Rice has to be over-cooked for better flavor and also for thick consistency.
2. In order to extract thick good quality coconut milk, use partly ripe coconut.
3. Some like to enjoy this with a pinch of salt, while others with sugar.
4. With no added sugar, with natural sweetness of coconut, this is a healthy dessert to have but in moderation.

# Panchakadai

## Lentil pudding

Panchakadai is a sweet dish, Ganesh Chathurthi Special

# Panchakadai – Lentil pudding

**Time**

45 Minutes

**Serves**

2-3 bowls

**Ingredients**

Chick peas and Moong dal/green lentils mixture – ½ cup

Fresh Coconut Grated – 1 ¼ cup

Jaggery/brown sugar – ¾ cup

Elaichi/ Cardamom powder – ½ teaspoon

Sesame Seeds/ Til – 2 tablespoons

**Method**

Melt jaggery with the little water and boil it till you get a thick syrup. Once the thick syrup is ready, add grated coconut into it and cook it to form a dry mixture or churna. Keep it aside to cool.

Wash the dal mixture and drain thoroughly. In a different pan, dry roast the dal mixture, till you get a nice aroma. Keep it aside to cool too.

On cooling, grind the dal mixture in a food processor, to a coarse powder.

Wash, drain water and dry roast the sesame/til seeds, till they splutter.

Transfer the dal powder, churna, sesame/til seeds and cardamom powder into a bowl and mix well and your panchkadai is ready.

Optionally, add a dash of pure ghee/clarified butter to give a nice flavor to the Panchkadai.

Panchakadai is now ready to be served.

**TIPS**
1. While roasting the dal, do not over-fry them else they would have a bitter taste.
2. You can store this in refrigerator and eat over the week.
3. One may add ¼ cup poha/beaten rice into the Panchakadai, while serving, for a variation.
4. One may replace jaggery with sugar or sugar substitutes.
5. Lentils have beneficial nutrients like fiber, protein, minerals and vitamins, they are still low in calories and contain virtually no fat. Lentils are excellent source of proteins from plant source. As a sweet, they should be eaten in moderation.

# Kele halvo

Banana pudding

# Kele halvo – Banana pudding

**Time**

15 minutes

**Serves**

2 bowls

**Ingredients**

Ripe bananas – 2

Sugar – ¾ cup

Elaichi/ Cardamom powder– ½ teaspoon

Ghee/Clarified butter – 2 tablespoons

**Method**

Slice the banana in an inch broad piece. Fry these in two tablespoon of ghee or clarified butter. If you do not have ghee, you could use unsalted butter as well.

Once the banana pieces are golden brown, add sugar and cardamom powder.

**TIPS**

1. This is simplest of the recipes for a dessert. Easiest way to convert over-ripe banana into a tasty treat for children.
2. Nendrapazham banana is commonly used for this recipe but you can use any type of banana.
3. You can use sugar substitutes instead of sugar.
4. Bananas are naturally sweet and can help curb your sweet tooth if you get that afternoon sugar craving. A 6-inch banana has minimal calories; about one-fourth of the calories you would get from a chocolate candy bar. Additionally, about half of the fiber content in bananas is soluble. When soluble fiber reaches your digestive tract, it absorbs water and slows digestion. Food is forced to sit in your stomach for a while; making one feels full and satiated. Alongside the high levels of potassium and vitamin B6, bananas also have good levels of vitamin C, magnesium and manganese. Bananas are literally a super food but should be eaten in moderation as a sweet.

Made in the USA
San Bernardino, CA
24 April 2016